The Future That Doesn't Work

Social Democracy's Failures in Britain

Edited by R. Emmett Tyrrell, Jr.

Samuel Brittan	Leslie Lenkowsky
Patrick Cosgrave	Harry Schwartz
Peter Jay	Colin Welch
Irving Kristol	James Q. Wilson

Peregrine Worsthorne

Most of the essays included in *The Future That Doesn't Work* originally appeared in *The Alternative: An American Spectator* magazine. The essays by Harry Schwartz, James Q. Wilson, and Peregrine Worsthorne also appeared, respectively, in *Medical Economics, The Public Interest,* and *Encounter.* A different version of Samuel Brittan's essay appeared in the *British Journal of Political Economy.*

University Press of America, Inc.

P.O. Box 19101, Washington, D.C. 20036

ISBN (Perfect): 0-8191-2740-X

The Future That
Doesn't Work

Contents

The Future That
Doesn't Work

Introduction

R. Emmett Tyrrell, Jr.

Since—roughly speaking—the first quarter of the nineteenth century, a powerful sense of cultural inferiority has crept into the realms of American leadership. This sense of inferiority (combined with shared customs) has given Europe, specifically England, a powerful influence over American life. The "progressive" ways of the English have been extolled throughout this century by Americans intent on conducting America along the British path, and so successful have these progressive Americans been that today most of our government expenditures go to institutions very similar to England's.

There has always been a whiff of the *opéra bouffe* lingering around the campaign to bring the institutions of British social democracy to these shores. The provincial earnestly denounces the hellishness of governmental programs, the cosmopolitan sniffs that no less a civilization than Great Britain has had such programs for years—and so the provincial collapses before a roar of ridicule from the trendies. Yet today the tactic of raising English social programs as an exemplar is little used, for along with its extensive social programs it also has about the lowest growth rate in the developed world, a straitened rate of productivity, and, of course, a deteriorating physical plant. Further, it has high inflation, high unemployment, and, as James Q. Wilson points out, a surprising amount of social unrest. The United

Kingdom has become the latest version of the Sick Man of Europe and, as the United States has been on a similar diet, one might well ask if this nation is fated to go the way of the United Kingdom, and what, if anything, can be done to duck such a fate.

Pertinent to answering these two questions is an inquiry into contemporary England's intellectual ancestry, for as Lord Keynes noted many years ago, "it is ideas, not vested interests, which are dangerous for good or ill." Social democratic ideas almost all spin off from the fundamental tenet that government must attend to every need of the citizenry, and England's social democrats have constantly enlarged the number of these needs. The cost of English government has so expanded that it now devours some 60 per cent of the nation's Gross National Product. To pay for it, the government has steeply raised taxes and steeply inflated the currency, inflation being the kind of arcane tax that politicians relish and voters fail to understand. This idea of expanding services, costs, taxes, and inflation is obviously not unheard of here in America. It prevailed during most of the 1960s and the early 1970s. The idea is not as well established here as in England, but neither are our rates of inflation and taxation. In fact, the other notions of England's social democrats are only now beginning to flower on these shores. I speak of the concepts that free enterprise is antediluvian, that profit is wicked, that achievers are exploiters, and that income—status, too, come to think of it—must be redistributed. All of these ideas have been vegetant in England for years, and Colin Welch has written eloquently of their English ancestry. Samuel Brittan and Peter Jay elucidate the complications inherent in social democracy, making it apparent that as the process matures, its attendant complications begin to overwhelm its democratic pretenses.

Ravening interest groups are a large complication. In

England the most grasping interest group has for years been the trade union movement, and Peregrine Worsthorne discusses the matter in an essay that should be particularly stimulating to an American audience, for if America has been blessed with more prudent and public-spirited trade unions, we have also been damned with an interest-group greed that closely parallels the evolution that Worsthorne discusses.

Social democrats are not given to frequent discussions of these complications, preoccupied as they are with their dream of a better world. That better world, distinguished by its lofty "quality of life," has long been the promise of British socialism, and so it is especially instructive to analyze some of the ingredients of social democracy's better world. Three of the major ingredients are nationalized health care, comprehensive welfare, and freedom from the social turbulence that social democrats so often associate with untidy capitalist systems. I have invited Harry Schwartz, Leslie Lenkowsky, and James Q. Wilson to review English performance in these areas. All are seasoned students of these affairs and speak with authority. Their discoveries would give Beatrice Webb and Norman Thomas hours of uneasy reading.

Yet one doubts that either the complications that British socialism has developed or the botches that it has bred are apt to lure social democrats away from their dream. They have heard it all before, and still they plunge on. In fact, Britain's decline into economic bankruptcy and political demoralization must be one of the most accurately and noisily predicted declines in world history. The Fabians were warned of the consequences of their schemes at the outset. From the Attlee government on, every step into the "better world" has been accompanied by warnings of economic peril followed closely by just that. And this makes the essays of Patrick Cosgrave and Irving Kristol so pertinent, if not for Britons, then for Americans.

In June of 1946 *The Economist* admonished Labour that "The human donkey requires either a carrot in front or a stick behind to goad it into activity. . . . The whole drift of British society for two generations past has been to whittle away both at the carrot and the stick, until now very little of either is left." In May of 1976 *The Economist* found that the carrot and the stick had all but disappeared. Britain's plight worsened, the pound took another fearful drubbing, and the Labour government again sought relief at the loan windows of the world's banks. That Labour shows feeble signs of mending its ways, of allowing enterprise its reward and profligacy its consequences, is obvious. But America still has time to question Britain's "progressive ways" and, if America does not, one might well ask to whose loan windows it will have access.

I should like to take this opportunity to thank all the authors who have contributed so thoughtfully to this collection, the many others who have favored me with their good counsel, and my colleague at *The Alternative*, Adam Meyerson, who was so tireless and rigorous in his work on these manuscripts.

The Trade Unions: New Lads on Top

Peregrine Worsthorne

"The miners are going to be at the top of the tree, and if that hurts somebody, I am sorry." Thus spake Mr. Joe Gormley, president of the National Union of Miners, in response to a national appeal by Britain's socialist government for common sacrifices in the fight against inflation.

Mr. Gormley is neither a militant nor an extremist, still less a Marxist. Quite the opposite. He stands out from his peers as being eminently reasonable, moderate, and responsible, a perfect model of a modern trade union leader, much respected, even loved, by the public at large for his human decency and earthy, Yorkshire common sense. Yet even this paragon, this most statesmanlike of trade union spokesmen, does not hesitate to use this kind of arrogant language; he is prepared, quite unashamedly, to admit to being brazenly and ruthlessly concerned about promoting a sectional interest, however this may "hurt" anybody else.

The easy explanation is that nowadays in Britain the trade union leaders, even the gentlest of them, are so powerful that they can afford to snap their fingers at public opinion, rather in the manner of Marie Antoinette telling the French people to eat cake in the absence of bread. Up to a point, of course, the trade unions *are* much stronger than they have ever been before. But they are not talking like this because they are more powerful. They are more powerful because they are talking like this, because they dare to talk like this.

And they dare to talk like this because, unlike the leaders of every other institution in Britain, they, and they alone, have a clear sense of their own value and an unshaken faith in their own function. Alone among the leaders of contemporary Britain they are totally unencumbered by a sense of guilt, and this uniqueness enables them to display a truly aristocratic disregard for public disapproval—a disregard so spectacularly provocative as to be literally awe-inspiring.

To understand the hegemony recently won by the trade unions in Britain, it is essential to start with this central insight: Their strength springs from a profound sense of moral legitimacy, the like of which is no longer shared by any other institution. They do not, properly speaking, have power. What they have, in a word, is *authority*. They are, in Britain, the embodiment of a commanding idea that has become, in recent years, invincible: the idea of social justice. Not, needless to say, the perfect embodiment. Very far from it, as I shall seek to show. But more of an embodiment of this commanding idea than any other institution, and in the Kingdom of the Blind, the one-eyed man is King.

A writer in the *Sunday Times* caught an aspect of this truth recently when he observed, after attending the 1975 trade union annual conference, that "trade unionists now wear the sort of ties and blazers that once marked out the public school man. As the middle classes let their hair grow and knot multicolored ties about their necks, the trade unionists keep their hair short and sport the stripes and badges of their union—a sure sign of a diminishing sense of identity in one group and an increasing assertiveness in the other."

These two aspects of the problem seem to me integrally connected, the *increasing* assertiveness of the trade unions being caused, or, if not altogether caused, certainly aggravated and encouraged, by the *decreasing* sense of identity among all the countervailing power groups in the land. Television illustrates this process almost every night. There can be no doubt that the most impressive personages to appear on the box nowadays are trade union leaders, since they are the only people who do not apologize for what they are doing, who do not seem to be embarrassed or ashamed by their role and purpose, and who are actually prepared to admit that, if necessary, they will exert their full strength to get what they want. "The lads need more money and they are bloody well going to get it." "All we ask is another £25 a week. Don't tell us the firm can't pay, since so long as the bosses drive around in Rolls-Royces that excuse is a lot of damned nonsense."

The message, of course, makes no economic sense. But given the contemporary obsession with social justice, nobody ever replies with equal bluntness, telling the workers to go and get stuffed. What the viewer sees are spokesmen for the working class confidently clenching their left fists, resisted by nothing more impressive than the soft underbelly of the bourgeoisie, quivering with guilt and apologizing for being rich (just as clergymen today always apologize for believing in God).

That is the point. Trade unions have a cause that excuses excess, or at any rate seems to render it understandable and even tolerable. Educated opinion does not approve of the unions' language or behavior, or the extent to which they bully society at large. There is a lot of tut-tutting and even indignation. But it is not wholehearted indignation, because however immoral some of the methods used by the trade unions are felt to be, their basic aim—improving the lot of working people—is still felt to be of almost religious significance. Just as Popes in the Middle Ages got away with murder, claiming to be doing God's work, so today do trade union leaders enjoy a comparable kind of immunity and protection, because they are doing the modern equivalent of God's work.

Another posh Sunday newspaper, for example, has just carried a long article by another miners' leader, Arthur Scargill, boasting of how, in the last miners' strike, in 1974, he led a mass picketing operation so militant, so numerous, and so passionately violent that it literally overpowered the police who sought to control it. The article is filled with the joy of battle and positively glories in trade union power, physical power ruthlessly deployed.

If a British general were to write about the battle against the IRA in Ulster with a comparably uninhibited display of pride and pleasure in the business of suppressing terrorism, or were to use the same kind of boastfully aggressive language about some successful military operation, he would be dismissed as a pathological case, a throwback to an age of barbaric imperialism. Let a police chief talk about the fight against crime with even so much as a hint of brutal determination and there would be an outcry of indignation from polite opinion. Liberal papers like the *Times* and the *Guardian* would yell for his resignation.

So deeply drenched in liberal squeamishness is respectable contemporary opinion in Britain that soldiers and policemen are expected to talk like Quaker brethren. It is recognized, reluctantly and grudgingly, that their function requires recourse to physical force. But on no account must they be seen to enjoy it, or to engage in it with zest and enthusiasm. If they are to be acceptable to the "powers that be," soldiers and policemen must approach their tasks with reluctant disdain and mournful apology, as if they were ashamed of being caught up in such savage pursuits. On television it is always they who are on the defensive, having to justify their actions, even to apologize for them, and the tiniest example of excessive severity is certain to lead to their instant dismissal and disgrace.

Trade union violence, on the other hand, enjoys a much wider degree of tolerance and provokes a much less absolutely hostile response. To suggest that it is approved of, or even tolerated, would be going too far. But liberal opinion reacts to violence in this area with ambivalence, with a desire to understand, and even with a certain sympathy, since fighting for workers' rights, albeit occasionally with excessive zeal, has come to seem more respectable, more glorious, more in keeping with the spirit of the age, than upholding the law or defending the realm.

How this came about I shall go into in a moment. But it is difficult to doubt, on the evidence, that it *has* come about. Take, for example, the furor about two building site pickets, known as the "Shrewsbury Two," who were sent to prison for using violence against nonunion workers, because they had refused to lay down tools during an industrial dispute—violence so extreme that one of the victims lost an eye. It was a horrible business. Nobody denies that extreme and extensive violence did take place. Even so, the trade union movement was and is indignant about the convictions, and there have been mass marches and demonstrations appealing for the release of the two thugs who now enjoy martyr status in the eyes of their fellow trade unionists. A few of the present members of the Labour government have publicly dissociated themselves from this trade union agitation, but most have not. While not lending it their overt support, they have been careful to avoid actually denouncing it.

To some extent this is sheer political expediency, not wanting to annoy the trade union movement at a time when its co-operation in wage restraint is being so actively courted. But that is not the whole explanation. More significant, in my view, is the deep-seated feeling by all members of the Labour Party that there *is* something indecent about sending workers to prison for any acts undertaken in pursuit of industrial disputes, however lawless or brutal the acts may have been. Nor is this just a working-class or Labour Party view. It is shared, to a lesser degree, by many middle-class Conservatives as well. Sending workers, *qua* workers, to prison is felt to be slightly shocking, unnatural, almost blasphemous, rather as in older times it would have seemed shocking and unnatural for the law to lay its hands on members of the nobility. Needless to say, this is not a universal view. There are some right-wingers who would like to see trade unionists hung, drawn, and quartered. But this kind of hostility is regarded as rather disreputable by the reigning liberal middle-class establishment, which today shows the same unmistakable signs of snobbishness toward, and deferential indulgence of, lower-class bad behavior as once it did of the bad behavior of the upper class.

If anybody doubts this, reflect for a moment on how inconceivable it would be for a great capitalist corporation, like ICI or Unilever, to organize a national campaign for the release of two of its directors caught red-handed in some thuggery comparable to that for which the "Shrewsbury Two" were convicted—bursting into a rival boardroom, say, and beating into a pulp a group of competitor directors who had refused to join in some cartel arrangement. It is even more inconceivable, in the event of such an agitation ever getting under way, that a Conservative government would refuse to condemn it or that some Ministers would lend it their support.

Needless to say, even the most purblind supporter of the capitalist cause would not feel prepared, let alone compelled, to defend thuggery or lawlessness of this kind, and still less to expect or demand that Conservative Ministers of the Crown should assist them in doing so. Such madness would spell the death of capitalism and the total discrediting of the Tory Party, since all sections of public opinion would be aghast, horrified, and totally repelled.

Yet these kinds of extraordinary goings-on do take place in the event of trade union thugs being sent to jail, and public opinion is not aghast, horrified, and totally repelled, or at any rate not remotely to the extent that it would be by comparable behavior on the part of any other power group. To the best of my knowledge, there have been no mass desertions from the trade union movement in protest of the obscene attempt to canonize these two thugs, or from the Labour Party for failing to anathematize this attempt. There have been critical articles in the liberal press, true, but no sense of national outrage as would certainly be provoked if any other power group were to behave with the same kind of shameless indecency.

The reason, of course, is very obvious. Trade unionists now enjoy a special dispensation, a unique exculpatory glamor that takes much of the sting out of public criticism. Mythologically speaking, they are still the underdogs, the underprivileged, with all the benefits that such a status bestows in an age dedicated to the cause of social justice. I am well aware of how absurd this is in present circumstances, since so many trade unionists are now the *nouveaux riches* and take home wage packets that make them the envy of professional people. In reality, the trade unionists are, for the most part, very far from being underdogs. Rather the reverse, as Conservatives try to point out.

But social attitudes never keep pace with reality, and it is really rather naïve to expect them to do so. It is, after all, only within the past quarter century that trade unionists have begun to exploit their economic strength to the full, and much of the adult British population had its attitudes formed during a period when the unions *were* the underdogs. This is still the impression that any British schoolboy would get from such historical lessons as he has at school, since this is how the trade unions are made to appear.

This, in itself, is a fascinating phenomenon—the extent to which the trade union movement, of all the institutions that flowered in the Victorian era, is the only one so far to have escaped the attention of historians bent on destroying favorable misconceptions, the only one that has not yet had its feet of clay exposed and its heroes demythologized. Imperialism, militarism, evangelicalism, Whiggism, Toryism, liberalism, and capitalism have all been debunked, but not trade unionism and its leaders. No Lytton Strachey, for example, has gotten to work on the great trade union leaders of the nineteenth century, showing them to be frauds and hypocrites, as has been done for the great soldiers, churchmen, statesmen, tycoons, etc.

Rather the opposite. The history of trade unionism is still told in reverential tones, with all the myths and legends of how the unions were oppressed and persecuted faithfully preserved. In fact, as revisionist historians will presumably soon get around to showing, the trade union leaders, even in the early days, were very far from being the heroic fighters for human rights that they are supposed to have been. Nor was their struggle for recognition nearly so uphill or so stony as they like to pretend.

It is fascinating to note, for example, that Frederic Harrison, the union nominee on the first Royal Commission set up to look into trade unionism in 1876, a man extremely well disposed toward the trade union cause, could not refrain from expressing his doubts in his private diary: "If the unions cannot get over it [violence against nonunion members], some of them, and certainly the masons, deserve all that was said of them and are as mere organs of class tyranny. My God! Think if I were to publish a formal recantation. But I keep my counsel as yet." In the event, he went on keeping his counsel, as a later entry shows: "I am not going to cave in now. The unions have serious faults but I still believe . . . them capable of improvement." This, as it turned out, was the general view of the Royal Commission, which produced majority and minority reports showing great sympathy and understanding of the union cause. What strikes one now, in looking back at the experience of British trade unionism in the nineteenth century, is not how hard it had to struggle against prejudice in high places, but how relatively quickly and easily it won its place in the sun.

But this is not the view taught in schools. At a time, as I say, when all the other British institutions have had their myths and legends stripped away, only the trade unions are still allowed to enjoy the benefit of brazen historical propaganda, in which they always appear as David fighting Goliath.

It is impossible to imagine, for example, the BBC commissioning a television series on the history of trade unionism that approached the subject in the same knocking spirit with which a recent BBC series approached the history of the British Empire; or to imagine a single prestigious filmmaker choosing to send up the language, customs, and rituals of, say, a mining village with the same derisory enthusiasm as a whole host of them regularly apply to the language, customs, and rituals of, say, a middle-class suburb or a stately home.

Not long ago, there was a splendid illustration of what I have in mind, in a BBC series "Days of Hope," which purported to dramatize the social conditions of England during and immediately after the First World War. We saw a young soldier deserter coming to the aid of a Yorkshire mining village during the 1921 coal strike, when the government of the day declared a national emergency and sent up the troops to maintain "law and order." There is no reason to complain about director Ken Loach's extreme bias in favor of the miners and against the coal owner, the

Army, and the police. That is his artistic right, and he
made the most of it.

But what is so interesting is that an artist of his high stature should have so absolutely uncritical an idea about a
mining village; should want to portray it in this sugary, sen-
timental, chocolate-box, and totally unrealistic way and see
nothing absurd in doing so, rather as, in an earlier age,
writers like G. A. Henty and Jeffrey Farnol saw nothing absurd in idealizing the British Army or in romanticizing the
British nobility. No reputable contemporary artist would
allow himself to be so naïvely indulgent about any other
group in society, or expect his public to tolerate such a
false perception. If he did he would be dismissed as a figure
of fun. Yet Ken Loach is taken very seriously indeed, since
the public does not want to be shown the naked truth about
working people. Their purity of heart, like that of the Victorian maiden, simply has to be assumed, even if this involves artistic nonsenses that will seem to succeeding generations no less incredible than the Victorian habit of
covering up the legs of pianos does to us.

Of course, this will change in time. But it has not
changed yet, and because it has not changed, contemporary
public opinion is indoctrinated in a wholly idealized and
glamorized picture of trade unionism, as an earlier public
was indoctrinated in a wholly idealized and glamorized picture of the aristocracy. And just as the idea of the aristocracy as a kind of divinely ordained topdog held sway over
the imagination of Englishmen long after it had ceased to
have any real basis in social or economic reality—long
after aristocrats, that is, had ceased to fulfill the function
from which their glamor originally sprang—so today the
glamor of the trade unions, as a kind of divinely ordained
defender of bottom dogs, continues to hold a comparable
place, although it, too, has no longer any basis in reality.

I have dwelt at some length on what must be called the

psychological background to trade union power, since it seems absolutely central to an understanding of the problem, at least as it affects Britain. Needless to say, the fundamental cause of increased trade union power has to do with the vulnerability of advanced, interdependent, postindustrial societies to the withdrawal of labor from certain vital industries, like energy. The trade unions, by ruthless use of the strike weapon for a few weeks, can reduce a country like Britain to chaos far more effectively than the Luftwaffe was ever able to do. This trade union power is common to all advanced economies where the right to strike is recognized. Yet only in Britain has this weapon been exploited to the full in recent years, to the point where an elected government, Mr. Edward Heath's, was destroyed by it. The questions that have to be answered are why the British trade unions feel so much more militant than do their counterparts in other Western countries and, equally interesting, why the rest of society shows such a strange apathy and weakness in the face of this challenge.

These questions, it seems to me, have to be answered in terms of class morale, by understanding the factors making for high working-class morale and low middle-class morale, even though such an analysis runs the risk of gross simplification. The cult of equality currently sweeping the Western world hit this country far harder than it did any other country, because there was so much more to hit: that is to say, so much more inequality. Not necessarily more inequality of wealth, but more inequality of lifestyles, manners, language, accents, appearances, and habits. The cult of equality has unsettled Britain more than any other country because its institutions were so inherently associated with the idea of inequality, with a class system rooted in inegalitarian ideas and values. One of the disadvantages of Britain is that, because of its record of continuity and its avoidance of political and social upheaval or revolution, all its institutions give the fatal impression of being far more stamped with a privileged style, with the manners and appearances of the *ancien régime,* than do those of, say, France or West Germany or, even more obviously, those of the United States. As a result, British institutions are particularly susceptible to being made to look provocatively out of keeping with the spirit of the times.

In no respect is this more obvious than in the confrontations between the two sides of industry, between management and labor. Although management, in the past decade or so, has in fact been vastly democratized, in the sense of being largely made up now of self-made men, it still does not give this impression, since its spokesmen sound and look posh, appearing in speech and dress much like gentlemen. However much they may struggle to escape the fatal appearance of inherited privilege, something of its patina still settles upon them. How could it be otherwise? A class system as deeply entrenched as Britain's has a momentum that carries on long after the engine has been switched off, and however much the new type of managers may spring from the same family background as the trade union leaders, the different educational and social experiences through which they have passed, on the way to the boardroom, mold them into the traditional boss-class shape, which is a shape that in modern times subtracts from, rather than adds to, their authority and confidence.

Britain in this respect suffers from a unique disadvantage. The successful self-made man cannot avoid moving into a life that associates him with a past social system that was rooted in inherited privilege, since the pattern of life at the top still dates from those days. Take the most obvious example of a country house. If a successful self-made tycoon wishes to indulge in such a purchase—or a successful Labour politician, for that matter—it is likely to involve him in the process of beginning to seem like a country gentleman or squire, with all the upper-class associations that go with such a status. Or if he joins a London club, it is likely to be a club that was originally a gentlemanly preserve full of echoes of the old ruling class. Britain has made enormous strides in the past quarter century toward the ideal of genuine equality of opportunity. In every walk of life the top prizes are increasingly open to men of talent. But much more than in any other country, this reality is disguised by a misleading image that suggests that little has changed, since the new nonhereditary ruling few are surrounded by the same symbols as were the old hereditary ruling few, thus fating them to share in the inhibitions and defensiveness that nowadays are the inevitable accompaniment of anything that smacks of privilege.

Only the trade union leaders, so far, have escaped this albatross and are therefore in a position to exercise power without apology, since they look and sound as men of power should look and sound in an age when privilege is a mark, not of divine grace—as it used to be—but of the devil's handiwork (much more so than Labour Party leaders who are increasingly indistinguishable, in social and educational background, from their Conservative counterparts). Not only, in short, do they have the increased economic power that, as I say, is a factor common to all trade union movements today in a free society; they also have this intangible advantage of embodying the one style of leadership in Britain today that avoids appearing both anachronistic and illegitimate. They are exceptionally strong, therefore, both physically and morally; so strong as to be, at any rate for the time being, irresistible.

I say "for the time being," since it is only a matter of time before the cultural worm begins to turn and starts eating away at working-class power and authority, as it has eaten away at the moral base of earlier power groups. But until this happens, until the breach is made between the wielders of physical power and the cultural legitimizers of that power, there is not much that can be done by those who would wish to reverse this trend.

In any case, those who do wish to reverse this trend—let us call them, for want of a better description, the conservative bourgeoisie—suffer from another disadvantage, also peculiar to Britain. They are, quite simply, much too nice —far nicer than their counterparts on the Continent or in the United States. This again is another hangover of the British class system which, through the public schools, taught the nineteenth-century bourgeoisie to think like country gentlemen. As a result, their heirs today find themselves locked in a chivalrous tradition wholly unsuited to the new reality of class war created by trade union militancy, rather as the medieval knights, accustomed to the romantic tournaments of Arthurian legend, were gravely inhibited when it came to fighting pitched battles against peasant armies.

Noblesse oblige and all the other anachronistic hangovers of an aristocratic age, which only make sense against a background of secure privilege and unchallenged strength, still debilitate the boardrooms of Britain, inducing in them a wholly inappropriate reluctance to recognize that the paternalistic days of benevolent goodwill have long since passed into history. The backs of British management are up against the wall; yet they still hanker after sitting on the fence, as if the fence itself had not been turned into a barricade.

In the bad old days of capitalistic exploitation, such a civilizing injection of a feudal sense of responsibility was thoroughly desirable, vastly and valuably moderating the ruthless inhumanity of class warfare. It was all to the good then that the bourgeois boss should have married into the landed gentry, been educated at an Anglican public school, and generally merged his identity in a way of life rooted more in the cricket fields of Eton than in the jungle of the marketplace; better, that is, at least in terms of social peace if not in terms of maintaining Britain's industrial supremacy.

But today, with the balance of power having switched overwhelmingly to the side of organized labor, these gentlemanly inhibitions, these anachronistic scruples born out of a world of green lawns and dreamy spires are proving an appalling handicap in the new cycle of class war about to reach its climax, since the trade union generals of the opposing armies—Jones, Scanlon, McGahey, Scargill—have learned their ethics of combat in an entirely different and more serious school where no holds are barred, no Marquis of Queensberry rules observed.

A deeply disturbing parallel can be drawn between the way this problem is now affecting us domestically and the way it bedeviled foreign affairs in the twenties and thirties, when the then ruling class proved pitifully unwilling to recognize the ruthless nature of the powers arrayed against it: the extent to which the new rulers in Japan, Germany, and Italy were fighting for supremacy in earnest, inhabiting a world that owed nothing to Christian pieties instilled in the classrooms and chapels of the English public school. Herr Hitler was not a gentleman. Nor are the Communists in the unions, who are fighting to win.

On the European Continent, the industrial climate is notably different from what it is in Britain, because management is backed by a middle class no less prone to explosions of militant anger, no more reluctant to take to the streets—yes, and to the barricades too, if necessary—than are the workers.

Take France, for example, where the middle class is fully prepared to march, demonstrate, and break windows— even heads, if need be—rather than allow itself to be pushed around or dictated to by the left. If on a Monday the Communists get a hundred thousand parading down the Champs-Elysées, hands clenched in menace, on a Tuesday the right will do the same. Each side knows the other's strength, and potential nastiness, and respects it. There is a real and chastening balance of mutual deterrence.

But that is because the bourgeoisie thinks like a bourgeoisie, with its values rooted in a proper understanding of what the class struggle entails, and its range of vision uninterrupted by the mirage of gentlemanly, turn-the-other-cheek behavior. In the heyday of high capitalism this was a great disadvantage, since it meant that the Continental bosses ground the faces of the poor with a primitive, single-minded savagery that the older aristocratic influence greatly helped to dilute in Britain. The result was Red revolution in France, from which Britain was spared.

But the problem today is not one of moderating the excesses of capitalism, at a time of pitiful proletarian weakness, for which purpose the English public school education, with its contempt for hard industrial efficiency and its romantic idealization of knightly chivalry, was so admirably suited. The problem today is one of resisting ruthless trade union power, of fighting for bourgeois values against overwhelming odds.

For this wholly different purpose the public school ethic is disastrously inappropriate, deplorably inhibiting. The Gentlemen of England would prefer to die rather than demonstrate, and a stiff upper lip, or, if driven to extremity, perhaps a rolled umbrella, is the nearest thing to an offensive weapon they would think of brandishing against the massed muscle of organized labor.

As a result, the social balance in Britain has been dangerously upset, with organized labor discovering the full extent of its power—which in any advanced technological society is almost limitless—and without any countervailing spirit of comparably aggressive purposefulness animating the other side of industry. The language and the mood of the right are still redolent of a vanished age when the middle class, unlike its Continental counterparts, felt so impregnably secure as to indulge in a kind of psychological disarmament that has now left it perilously vulnerable.

No doubt this too will change, in time. But I am writing of the present, not the future, trying to explain why the trade unions *today* are riding so high in Britain. There are many other reasons than those which I have touched on here. But the most basic reason, which I have tried to describe, is that their rise to a position of economic ascendancy, brought about largely through the accidents of technological development, has coincided with social and cultural developments that enable them to use their strength with a clear conscience, while those who would resist them lack the will to do so uninhibitedly, because they doubt—or feel guilty about—the virtue of their cause. To some extent, all this is true of other capitalist societies. But it is more true in Britain than elsewhere, which is why the problem is so much worse there and will take so much longer to solve.

The Infirmity of British Medicine

Harry Schwartz

There was a time not so long ago when would-be reformers of the American medical system enthusiastically pointed to Britain's National Health Service as an example to be emulated in this country. Britain had proved, we were told, that a socialized medical system could work, and work well. And the British people, we were informed, were so satisfied with the NHS that no British politician of any party would ever dare tamper with it.

A more realistic note has crept into American discussion of the subject in recent months, as graphic front-page headlines—"BRITAIN'S HEALTH SERVICE TO UNDERGO INVESTIGATION"; "BRITISH HOSPITALS HIT BY SLOWDOWN OF YOUNG DOCTORS"—have begun to dispel the illusions of idyllic British health care. But in Britain, amid the shambles of their economy and their political system, many prominent observers now openly acknowledge that the chickens have come home to roost for their health service. Consider the disillusionment of Dr. David Owen, the Labour Minister in day-to-day charge of the NHS, as expressed in a recent interview with the London *Sunday Times*:

"The health service was launched on a fallacy. First we were going to finance everything, cure the nation and then spending would drop. That fallacy has been exposed. Then there was the period when everybody thought the public could have whatever they needed on the health service—it was just a question of governmental will. Now we recognize that no country, even if they are [sic] prepared to pay the taxes, can supply everything."[1]

These were commendably honest admissions for the socialist head of a socialized medical system. In effect, Dr. Owen conceded that a generation's experience tended to confirm the fears conservative economists had expressed when the NHS was first being debated and fought over. In that same interview Dr. Owen also spoke of great inequalities in the health services available to the people of Britain, and of the existence of "quite severe areas of health deprivation" even in the otherwise favored London metropolitan region. He called Newham, a town near London, "an appallingly deprived area."

Or consider these recent criticisms by Bernard Dixon, editor of the British magazine *New Scientist*: "The plight of Britain's Health Service conflicts desperately with the avowedly utopian ideals of its founders. Yet the myth persists —the myth that the NHS not only can but does offer a high and unvarying level of medical care to all members of the community. For most of us, it is only when we join a year-long hospital waiting list, or have to take an injured child to a hospital casualty department on Sunday afternoon, that we realize just how threadbare and starved financially the service really is." Mr. Dixon added: "Not only is there an acute shortage of resources, but the expertise and facilities that are available are all too often dispensed via a conveyor-belt system which can at times be positively inhuman."[2]

To judge these and other current expressions of dissatisfaction, we must go back to the origins of the National Health Service and trace, even if only briefly, its development over the past three decades. The NHS began in 1948, but its working plans were devised during World War II, when all Britons shared a common fate and a common danger. In the Beveridge Report of 1942, an "ideal plan" was proposed, "a health service providing full preventive and curative treatment of every kind for every citizen without exceptions, without remuneration limit and without an economic barrier at any point to delay recourse to it." As the *British Medical Journal* commented at the time, this was to be "a 100 per cent service for 100 per cent of the population."[3]

Prime Minister Winston Churchill, absorbed in his wartime task of rallying the British people to ever greater exertions and sacrifices, was doubtless glad to have a glittering prize to offer his people for the postwar period. He added to the rhetoric: "The discoveries of healing science must be the inheritance of all: That is clear. Disease must be attacked whether it occurs in the poorest or the richest man or woman, simply on the ground that it is the enemy; and it must be attacked in the same way that the fire brigade will give its full assistance to the humble cottage as it will give it to the most important mansion. . . . Our policy is to create a national health service, in order to secure that everybody in the country, irrespective of means, age, sex, or occupation, shall have equal opportunities to benefit from the best and most up-to-date medical and allied services available."[4]

Given such verbiage from the leader of Britain's Conservative Party, there is no need to present the rosy vistas opened up by Labour politicians. Suffice it to recall that Aneurin Bevan, who piloted National Health Service legislation through Parliament and then supervised initial organization and operation of the NHS, referred in one parliamentary debate to his conviction "that we ought to take pride in the fact that despite our financial and economic anxieties, we are still able to do the most civilized thing in the world—put the welfare of the sick in front of every other consideration."[5]

As the quotations from Dr. Owen and Mr. Dixon indicate, the rhetoric of the 1940s has long been discredited. Britain does not today "put the welfare of the sick in front of every other consideration," nor has Churchill's goal of "equal opportunities to benefit from the best and most up-to-date medical and allied services available" been realized. Of all the factors involved in these disappointments, cost has undoubtedly been one of the most important. Yet it is clear that the politicians who launched the National Health Service were little concerned about cost. In a revealing discussion, Bevan's biographer—present Labour Party Cabinet member Michael Foot—reports that the father of the NHS attached little importance to advance estimates of cost. Such estimates were bound to be guesswork, and Bevan said: "The true provision for a free health service must depend on the behaviour of the public, and the only way to discover it must be to permit the public to behave! A year's practical working of the scheme would be needed to discover the cost with real accuracy."[6]

More fundamentally, Bevan was the victim of a colossal misconception, implied by Dr. Owen's admission of the "fallacy" on which the NHS was launched: "We were going to finance everything, cure the nation and then spending would drop." Bevan believed that a large amount of sickness in Britain resulted from insufficient medical care. Under the NHS, he reasoned, the sick would get well as soon as they were properly treated. Then costs would drop. Once, when a British Medical Association leader asked him, "What, Mr. Bevan, is your long-term prospect and hope for members of the profession?" his reply was: "A high incidence of unemployment."[7]

In his 1952 political autobiography *In Place of Fear*, Bevan stated his misconception clearly: "When the Service started and the demands for spectacles, dental attention and drugs rocketed upwards the pessimists said: 'We told you so. . . .'

"Ordinary men and women were aware of what was happening. They knew from their own experience that a considerable proportion of the initial expenditure, especially on dentistry and spectacles, was the result of past neglect. When the first rush was over, the demand would even out."[8]

Now we know that Bevan was wrong. The demand does not "even out." The patient who is cured today lives to get sick tomorrow, and the older he gets the more likely he is to become the victim of a serious, disabling ailment requiring long and expensive treatment. Nor did Bevan foresee the rapid progress of medical technology, which provided new means of curing the sick and easing or eliminating disability, but often—as in the case of kidney transplants and open-heart surgery—at very high cost. Most fundamentally, he did not understand that if patients need not pay directly for medical care, they will resort to it for the trivial indisposition as well as for the serious illness, and there is no end to the demands of those an American physician has called "the worried well." As Conservative politician Enoch Powell formulated it, in what has come to be known as Powell's Law, the demand for "free" medical care quickly outruns any possible provision for it.

It did not take long, in any case, for the ogre of cost to make its appearance. Already in the first months of the NHS operations Bevan had to make several public appeals against abuse of the service, for as Michael Foot has written, ". . . the demand was exceeding anything he had dreamt of." The costs of health care soon began to provoke serious political conflicts within the Labour government, for example in February 1949, when it became known that £52 million (an enormous sum of money then) would be required in excess of original budget estimates to meet NHS costs.[9]

These conflicts came to a head in the spring of 1951, when Bevan resigned from the Labour government after his Cabinet colleagues decided to establish charges for eyeglasses and false teeth. The argument was, as always, about priorities. The charges would save the government an estimated £23 million, and Bevan's chief opponent, Hugh Gaitskell, reasoned that this money would be better spent on old-age pensions than on free glasses and dentures. It was becoming clear that the needs of the NHS were in direct competition with the defense budget, old-age pensions, government investment in housing, and all the other multifarious demands on the limited resources of the British Government. And Bevan's resignation signified that even his Labour colleagues were not prepared to give the NHS the overriding top priority he had told the nation it would get.

In fact, Britain's political leaders—both Labour and Conservative—soon learned that the only way to cope with the overwhelming demand for "free" medical services was to impose a ceiling on total NHS expenditure. Forgotten was the heady talk about everybody having all the latest medical aid he or she might need when he or she needed it. Instead there was the hardheaded realization that resources could not be used if they were not available. And if that meant shortages and people being forced to wait for months or even years, so be it. The British people, famous for their patience, for their willingness to queue up for buses or for whatever else they had to wait for, could queue up as well for nonemergency medical care.

What was worse, the political and economic pressures on the NHS led to budgetary decisions by both Labour and Conservative governments which, over the long run, only aggravated the shortages and deficiencies of British medical care. There is a limit even to British patience, and the almost endless demand for "free" services quickly translated into political clamorings for more of them. As the British economists John and Sylvia Jewkes pointed out over twelve years ago: "What happened under these conditions was what was likely to happen. Governments followed the line of least resistance. They laid emphasis on those medical items which constituted pressing day-to-day demand, yielded their results quickly and with some certainty, made something of a public splash and conformed with the doctrine of equality. Conversely they tended to neglect those times where spending would bring only slowly maturing results, where economy would not be quickly noticed and therefore would be less likely to arouse public opposition. . . .

"These were the conditions under which preventive medicine, new hospitals and medical schools, occupational health services and medical research were likely to give way to a free supply of drugs, of doctors' services and of hospital care. However anxious a government might be to take a longer view, its resolve was likely to be weakened by the pressure of immediate demands; and by the hope that easier times were coming; that perhaps next year defense expenditures would be smaller, or investment needed for other purposes would be less, or the national income would rise sharply."[10]

One of the reasons often cited for nationalizing British health care was the need to modernize and expand Britain's antiquated hospital system. But as it turned out, a bias against capital investment was built into the structure of the National Health Service, so that doctors continue to treat patients in nineteenth-century hospitals, and the number of hospital beds per capita has actually declined. (In 1949 there were some 43 million people in England and Wales, and an average of 397,600 occupied NHS hospital beds. In 1974, there were about 49 million people, but only 420,942 available hospital beds.[11]) The Jewkeses calculated that per capita hospital construction expenditures were *six times as great* in the United States between 1950 and 1959 as they were in England and Wales during the first thirteen years of the NHS. And the problem, the Jewkeses observed, was not simply a capital shortage:

"The excuse usually given, that Britain was short of capital after the war is not convincing; the point is that other demands for public investment were rated high above that for the National Health Service. The reason seems to have been that successive Chancellors of the Exchequer, trying to keep down total expenditure on the Service by fixing a ceiling, threw the brunt of the saving upon those items where the consequences in the short period would be least noticeable and least likely to arouse protest."[12]

This penny pinching in capital investment has had many unfortunate consequences for the quality of health care, one being insufficient medical equipment. British general practitioners rarely have any medical instruments except for stethoscopes and blood-pressure cuffs; they must send their patients to hospitals even for chest X-rays and simple blood tests. Hospitals are not much better. Few funds are available, for example, for kidney grafts or dialysis machines, and many patients requiring kidney treatment have nowhere to turn for help. Perhaps a more striking example is the fact that as late as 1976 there were in all of Britain fewer than two dozen EMI brain scanners, remarkable machines that have revolutionized the diagnosis of brain disease and brain injuries, while there were hundreds in the United States (and these machines were invented and produced in Britain).[13]

The worst consequence, however, is the interminable waiting, caused by the shortage of hospital beds and doctors and surgeons. In December 1974, the NHS had a list of 517,000 people in England alone waiting for what was officially called noncritical surgery. Many of these people will have to wait years for care they want and need, and horror stories about the effects of such delays abound in the British medical literature. An open-heart operation is twice postponed for a Welsh woman, because there is no bed for her in the intensive-care unit; she dies at home shortly thereafter.[14] A sixty-six-year-old man suffers a stroke but is denied admission to the nearest hospital because no one over sixty-five is supposed to be treated there.[15] One hospital actually had twenty *unconscious* patients on its admissions waiting list, and "sent a trained health visitor round to assess the priority of these cases presumably to see who was the most unconscious."[16]

Judged by these lights, the British National Health Service is hardly a model for American medical care. In 1974, Britain spent about $7 billion on the NHS, while Americans, with somewhat less than four times Britain's population, spent well over $100 billion on health care-related activities. This difference is so overwhelming that it reduces to insignificance the purely statistical cautions against such a comparison, for example the difference in definitions of health care in the two countries. And while American medicine is often extravagant and wasteful, extravagance certainly does not account for the approximately *fourfold* difference in per capita medical spending between the United States and Britain. The fact is that by American standards, the NHS is a meager and Spartan medical system many of whose economies would be regarded as inhuman brutality if applied to Americans.

The differences between British and American health care go beyond mere spending differences, however. There seems much good sense in the recent judgment expressed by Dr. Dermot B. O'Brien, an Irish physician from Dublin Medical School who has worked in both the United States and Britain: ". . . the British people—whether as a result of different life philosophy or generally lower level of affluence—have a much lower level of expectation from medical intervention in general. In fact, they verge on the stoical as compared with the American patient, and, of course, this fact makes them, purely from a physician's point of view, the most pleasant patients. The resulting service has evolved over the years into a service that would in my opinion be all but totally unacceptable to any American not depending on welfare for medical services."[17]

Let us turn now to a somewhat more detailed look at the National Health Service, which is really two medical systems, linked but for all practical purposes separate. One system consists of family doctors who practice solo or in small groups. A British family signs up with a local general practitioner, and then, theoretically, its members can see him as often as they want. The GP is obliged to pay house calls whenever they are sufficiently urgent, and to be available to his patients every hour of the day and night and every day of the year; if he goes away on vacation, he is responsible for finding (and paying) a locum to replace him. The patient pays nothing out of pocket for this access, and the GP is compensated by the government under a complicated formula whose main ingredient is a capitation payment, so much annually per patient on his list. The doctor who wants to maximize his income thus has an incentive to get the largest possible list of subscribers—some doctors have well over three thousand patients—and to do as little as possible for each in order to save time and be able to serve the largest number of people.

Man does not live by bread alone, however, and the British Government has had to accept and cope with the fact that many doctors want to live in the most pleasant parts of the country—for example, in London or its suburbs—even if that means accepting the economic penalty of a smaller income from a shorter list. The government has sought to distribute GPs more evenly among patients by discouraging and even prohibiting young doctors from settling in "restricted areas" where authorities have decided there are enough or too many doctors. Similarly, the government pays bonuses to doctors willing to settle in "designated areas" where there is judged to be a shortage of GPs. In the twenty-seven years of the NHS, there has been some progress toward a more equal distribution of GPs throughout the country, but a recent study indicates that much more progress is needed.[18]

Supporters of the NHS see the availability of a personal family doctor for most Britons as a great achievement. They argue that these physicians take care of most minor and self-limiting physical illnesses and that they provide at least part of the psychological support for those patients with emotional problems. It is argued, moreover, that since access to a doctor is available without charge, patients' serious ills can be caught early when they are more likely to be curable. There is some truth to these arguments, and many Britons seem to be quite satisfied with this arrangement.

Critics, however, dismiss the general practitioners as quacks who quickly lose their original professional skills and become mere hand holders and tranquilizer prescribers because they never see any serious illness. As mentioned earlier, most British GPs have only the most primitive equipment and facilities. But the worst aspect of the system is the doctors' huge burden of work, especially in "designated areas": The GPs have so many patients that they must practice a mechanical and minimal kind of medicine. They see each patient for a very few minutes, give him a rushed examination, and prescribe something that they hope will hold him until his problem vanishes. Patients often complain that where GPs require appointments, the secretaries are instructed to try to discourage patients from coming in. The GP in turn complains that many patients plague him unnecessarily, and he feels it is bitterly unfair that he is always expected to be available to them.

In discussing British GPs, we are talking about roughly twenty-six thousand doctors ministering to several tens of millions of patients, about a quality of medicine that varies from the excellent, personalized, compassionate, and technically superb to uncaring travesties of health care, sometimes delivered by a foreigner whose English is none too good and who dislikes his patients as much as they dislike him. In such a complex situation, excessive generalization is unwise. Suffice it to note that GPs have successfully retained their right to see private patients, who pay directly for consultations, unlike NHS patients. Whether through greater courtesy, longer and more careful examinations, a more sympathetic reception, or—most likely—some combination of these considerations, private patients are convinced they get better care when they pay their general practitioner. Certainly a British GP whose office I visited saw his thirty or so NHS patients very quickly, giving them each one to four minutes, as timed on my watch. But he saw his single private patient for a full half hour.

The second part of the NHS is the hospital service, which generally consists of a series of personal empires, of lordly consultants who are specialists in different fields and who have lower-ranked doctors—many of them in their thirties and even some in their forties—serving under them. It is interesting that the consultant and his underlings are known as a "firm" and that the consultant is supreme in his medical empire, secure in his job for life, and accountable to almost no one. When a patient becomes seriously ill and must enter a hospital, he normally loses contact with his GP and is transferred to the care of one of these consultants and his staff of junior doctors.

The consultant and his staff also give outpatient consultations for patients referred by GPs. And though they are government employees, the consultants may also engage in private practice, a lucrative privilege many of them use and treasure. This is the result of a compromise reached between the consultants and Aneurin Bevan at the very birth of the NHS, a compromise reminiscent of that which Stalin reached with Soviet collective farmers in the early 1930s. Stalin moderated the peasants' objections to collectivization by allowing them to have their own small garden plots on which they could keep some livestock and grow produce to sell at high prices in free markets. Similarly British consultants are allowed to accept a 9/11 contract, a legal fiction that gives them only nine elevenths of a full-time consultant's salary while allowing them to see private patients and accept fees. But the legal responsibilities of both full-time and part-time consultants to their NHS patients are identical and total. In 1973, 49 per cent of all consultants had part-time contracts and saw private (paying) patients. Eighty per cent or more of all consultant ophthalmologists, general surgeons, otolaryngologists, orthopedic surgeons, and obstetricians and gynecologists see private patients. On the other hand, less than 20 per cent of all consultants in geriatrics, pathology, and mental retardation do so. Surgeons and anesthetists earn most of the private fees. In 1971–72 the average part-time consultant earned £8,354, of which £2,755 came from private practice, while the average full-time consultant earned £7,077.[19]

In addition to enjoying higher income, part-time consultants also gain income tax advantages because they can deduct the costs of earning the extra private fees. General practitioners—who are considered independent contractors, not government employees—also enjoy these tax advantages. Full-time consultants, who receive only salaries, do not. In Britain, where income taxes are very high, these tax advantages are even more appealing than in the United States.

Two more portions of this historic compromise must be mentioned. Bevan promised that a small number of beds would be reserved in NHS hospitals for private patients and that these would be under the control of the consultants. In 1974 there were 4,500 pay beds in England and Wales out of a total of about 420,000 beds. Bevan also set up a system of bonuses to be paid to consultants on the basis of merit. In 1974 about one third of all consultants received distinction awards worth from £1,500 (more than half of all awards) to almost £8,000 (to only 112 recipients). The result of this system of awards is that some consultants get very high incomes, for those who get the very highest awards are also likely to have the most lucrative private practices. Simultaneously, however, the majority of British consultants do not get any bonuses, and many of them are convinced that they have been unfairly denied extra compensation. But from the government's point of view this has the useful result of keeping tensions and jealousies high among consultants.

The essential question is why every year tens of thousands of British citizens pay fees to consultants (as private patients) when those same consultants are theoretically available free of charge through the NHS. Some private patients pay out of their own pockets. Some come from the ranks of the more than 2 million British citizens who belong to private health-insurance plans that pay fees for private consultations and also pay for the cost of NHS private beds in hospitals.

An eminent British surgeon who was then Regius Professor of Surgery at Oxford explained to me some years ago why so many persons resorted to private medicine even though "free" government medicine was available to them: "They value their health and their lives. Also they put a value on their convenience and they don't want to wait. When they come to me they know I'm the top expert and I'm giving them the benefit of my knowledge and experience. I spend time with them in consultation. When they're to be operated on, I do the operation and I take care of them after the surgery. I can arrange for them to be operated on quickly, maybe a few days or one or two weeks after the initial consultation. But on the National Health they have to take whatever junior person they get assigned; they don't know who's going to operate on them, and they realize the chances of getting me are slim. And they have to wait months or longer for the operation. So what they get when they pay is courtesy, time, my personal expert care, and the convenience of having the problem taken care of quickly. Don't you think that's worth paying for?"

The availability of private, paid care for British patients since the beginning of the NHS shows that the alleged goal of equality was abandoned at the outset of the enterprise. Obviously patients would pay neither general practitioners nor consultants if they did not believe that they were getting better medical care than they would have received as nonpaying NHS patients. In 1974 and 1975 more militant elements of the Labour Party began agitating for the abolition of private practice. A resolution demanding this abolition was passed at the 1975 annual conference of the British trade union movement. In 1974 unionized maintenance workers, nurses, and other nonphysicians attempted to wipe out private practice in some hospitals. For varying periods of time, they announced, they would not serve patients in private beds, hoping literally to starve those patients out of the hospitals. Much was made of the private patients' "queue jumping," that is, their ability to enter a hospital and to be operated on quickly and conveniently rather than waiting in line months or years. Under these pressures, the Labour Party platform in the last election campaign promised that if returned to power, the Wilson government would eliminate private beds from NHS hospitals. To the consultants, of course, this looked like a unilateral renunciation of the historic compromise by which Bevan had bought the consultants' agreement to participate in the NHS in 1948. The consultants' discontent was further sharpened in mid-1975 when it became plain that the Wilson government planned not only to eliminate private beds from NHS hospitals, but also to make it virtually impossible to build any significant number of private hospitals to replace the NHS private beds. All this helped provoke the consultants' slowdown in late 1975. The Wilson government denied that it planned to eliminate all private practice, but many consultants suspected that this was precisely what Prime Minister Wilson, Mrs. Barbara Castle— the Minister for Health and Social Security—and Dr. Owen were planning. Those suspicions were heightened when a government memorandum was "leaked" to the medical press. The memorandum outlined a scheme for relocating all general practitioners into government-operated health centers and then prohibiting the GPs from seeing private patients in these centers. The Wilson government, of course, promptly denied that it had any such intentions.

Most of the difficulties the NHS experienced in December 1975, however, came from the junior hospital doctors, the consultants' subordinates, rather than the consultants. These junior doctors had been promised overtime pay for work in excess of forty hours a week. (Many of them worked over one hundred hours a week, and it was their willingness to do so that had made the NHS possible since 1948.) But when it came time to pay them, the junior doctors discovered that all that was contemplated was a redistribution among them of the same total funds, with money added to the salaries of some often simply deducted from the salaries of others who had little or no opportunity to work long hours. The junior doctors retaliated in many hospitals by closing down emergency rooms after 5 P.M., but in many such institutions consultants—despite their own grievances—went on duty to make some emergency medical service possible. Nevertheless, it was clear that morale among physicians in the NHS was extremely low, and newspaper accounts referred freely and often to the "breakdown" or the "collapse" of the NHS.

Space limitations prevent us from considering other important aspects of the NHS. We have not, for example, even mentioned the very heavy dependence of NHS hospitals on Asian, African, and Caribbean doctors, many of them poorly trained. Just how poor their training is did not become fully evident—and a matter of public knowledge—until after mid-1975. At that time, newly arrived doctors were first given qualifying tests in medical knowledge and in ability to communicate in English. Of the hundreds tested in the first six months these examinations were given, only about one third passed. By inference, these results provided shocking information about the competence of foreign doctors who had been permitted for many years to work in hospitals without being tested. But in Britain the main question, as test after test produced calamitously high failure rates, was how long the NHS could continue to be even minimally staffed if two thirds or more of arriving Third World doctors were found ineligible for hospital posts. By early December 1975, the *British Medical Journal* was raising the question of when the standard of clinical knowledge required in the tests might have to be lowered to produce adequate numbers of foreign doctors for NHS hospitals.[20]

Nor have we raised the question of how first-rate medical care can be given to the people of England and Wales when there are so few specialists. At the end of 1974, according to the 1974 report of the Department of Health and Social Welfare, there were only 95 consultants in cardiology, 181 in dermatology, 36 in infectious diseases, 15 in nuclear medicine, 134 in neurology, 82 in neurosurgery, 77 in plastic surgery, 180 in radiotherapy, and 111 in thoracic surgery. These are ridiculously low figures for a population of 50 million, and they show that the old promises that everyone would have access to the best possible medical care are not being kept.

But we are now in a position to pronounce some judgments on the National Health Service. Medical care in Britain is better in the mid-1970s than it was thirty years ago. In Britain as in all other countries, the sick now have the important advantages gained from progress in medical science since the mid-1940s. And Britain is much richer now than it was in 1945 and 1948, so it has more doctors, both general practitioners and specialists, than it had when the NHS started. But the same progress has taken place in all Western countries, and British medical care would be much better today than in the 1940s even if the NHS had never been formed.

The real test of the National Health Service is twofold, at least if we are to measure it by the promises made originally. Has it achieved equality of medical care for all in Britain regardless of who they are or where they live? The answer here is obviously no, a negative reply that the present British Labour government accepts as much as its opponents do. Second, has the NHS made available the best of modern medicine to the sick in Britain? Again the answer is mainly negative. Those who have access to treatment in the London teaching hospitals and in a rather small number of similar hospitals in other parts of the country probably do get good care, but the great majority of the NHS clients live in areas with inadequate numbers of hospital beds, grossly deficient numbers of medical and sur-

gical specialists, and inadequate and outmoded medical
equipment.

With the wisdom of hindsight we can see that the NHS is
foundering on two rocks that could have been anticipated
even in 1948. One rock is the conflict over "equality." In
every society one of the most highly prized rewards for out-
standing work, talent, position, and accomplishment is
prompt access to superior medical care with all possible
amenities. Mao Tse-tung got far better medical care than a
Hunan peasant, just as Leonid Brezhnev gets better care
than a Ukrainian factory worker. There is no full equality
in access to medical care anywhere, nor can there be so
long as human societies must depend upon differential rewards to provide incentives. Nevertheless, the utopian Labour Party dream of "equality" has already gravely injured
the National Health Service and may yet cripple it even
more.

The second difficulty is that the successes of past, present, and future medical research all tend to make medical
care more expensive, and will probably continue to do so.
The potential demand for care—including psychiatric care,
the effort to develop the full potential of the severely re-
tarded, and the effort to give geriatric patients the benefit
of all possible help—can bankrupt any nation that attempts
to provide it free of charge. Britain tried to circumvent this
difficulty by keeping a tight lid on NHS expenditures, especially for fixed capital. But now even this is inadequate,
and the Labour government proclaims openly that it will
have to adopt an even more stringent system of priorities.
This must come down to the decision that some shall be
helped at the cost of others being permitted to die before
they need to. The conflicts on this issue have only begun,
but there can be no doubt that they will be fierce indeed
when the Draconian nature of the alternatives is fully realized. A rational solution would be to end the effort to real-

ize a completely socialized and "free" medical service and to permit the introduction of a much larger private sector to help share the cost. Perhaps some future British Government will have the courage to turn to this solution. Until then, continued deterioration of morale among key NHS staff and worsening provision of physical facilities for treating the sick seem unavoidable.

Intellectuals Have Consequences

Colin Welch

The fish, so the French say, decays from the head first. This is what justifies any study of the British left-wing intellectual. By "intellectual" I do not mean an intelligent person, who need not be either left-wing or strictly an intellectual. What I do mean is a person who thinks himself to be moved primarily or solely by his intellect (which may of course be very feeble or very powerful), who regards himself as an intellectual and makes a living thereby or, unable to do so, is influenced by those who do, in the columns of the *New Statesman* and elsewhere. Such people standing as they do in our recent history predominantly on the left, I expect the epithet "left-wing" to be understood wherever I use the word "intellectual"—and "British," too, for I am not qualified to write of others.

And if I pay a lot of attention to comparatively dull dogs like Sidney and Beatrice Webb, Harold Laski, John Strachey, R. H. Tawney, and Anthony Crosland, this is not because I think them more amusing than their wilder sidekicks but because I am sure they and their innumerable followers have had more influence. Despite the fact that only one of those I have mentioned, Mr. Crosland, is still alive,* Britian is still governed by them, perhaps increasingly so. They are still the brains of the ruling Labour Party; they have supplied its dominant prejudices and reflexes as well as the broad mass of its reasoning. Some oaf

---

* Anthony Crosland died of a stroke on February 19, 1977, just as this book went to press.

shrieks, "Shoot the bosses!" or "Make the rich squeal!" It appears to come from the natural promptings of an embittered and unlettered heart. Yet dimly behind such outbursts we are aware of the prompting and blessing of some remote gray ideologue, half forgotten yet still potent.

In trying to describe the intellectual I am daunted to find how much of my work was done for me nearly forty years ago by George Orwell, one of the breed himself for all his percipience and humanity, in *The Road to Wigan Pier*.

The typical socialist is not for him a ferocious worker with a raucous voice; no, it is either a youthful snob Bolshevik or, more typically, a prim little white-collar job man, possibly a teetotaler or vegetarian of nonconformist background, who has no intention of forfeiting his social position: both "unsatisfactory or even inhuman types."

Orwell wonders about the motives of the tract-writing intellectual. Love of the working class, from which he is so far removed? Hard this for Orwell to believe: more likely a "hypertrophied sense of order." He sees in Shaw, for instance, a dull, empty windbag who knows and cares nothing about poverty, who thinks it must be abolished from above, by violence if necessary—perhaps preferably by violence: hence Shaw's worship of "great" men, of dictators fascist or Communist, of Stalin and Mussolini.

Foaming denouncers of the bourgeoisie; book-trained intellectuals who want to throw what remains of our great but half-wrecked civilization down the sink, preferring a mechanized socialist future of "iron and water"; the more-water-in-your-beer reformers, Shaw the prototype; the astute young literary climbers who are Communists because it is fashionable; "and all that dreary tribe of high-minded women and sandal wearers and bearded fruit-juice drinkers who come flocking toward the smell of progress like bluebottles to a dead cat": all these are the freaks who, in Orwell's view, have brought socialism into disrepute. And, to

THE CAST

Beveridge, William Henry (1879–1963) was director of the London School of Economics and Political Science from 1919 to 1937, and afterward master of University College, Oxford. Active as a progressive publicist and in government ministries, his wartime report, *Social Insurance and Allied Services* (1942), set down the framework for the postwar welfare state. Beveridge wrote a number of other books, including *Planning Under Socialism* (1936) and *Full Employment in a Free Society* (1944), an influential economic treatise. In 1946 he was made Baron of Tuggal.

Crosland, Anthony (b. 1918), Foreign Secretary in the Callaghan government, has held many high positions in Labour administrations, among them President of the Board of Trade and Secretary of State for the Environment. Crosland, who has taught economics at Trinity College, Oxford, and who was chairman of the Fabian Society, is considered to be one of the most flexible and undoctrinaire leaders of the Labour Party. In *The Future of Socialism* (1956), he outraged the party's "left wing" by arguing against wholesale nationalization, occasionally praising capitalism and market economics, and suggesting that the party was tied too exclusively to the working class. His other books include *Britain's Economic Problem* (1953), *The Conservative Enemy* (1962), and *Socialism Now and Other Essays* (1974).

Johnson, Hewlett (1874–1966), Dean of Canterbury from 1931 to 1963, was known as the "Red Dean" for his frank Communist sympathies. His many books include *Soviet Success* (1947), *China's New Creative Age* (1953), and *The Upsurge of China* (1961). In 1939, after the Soviet Union concluded its nonaggression pact with Germany, Johnson was quoted as saying: "Communism has recovered the essential form of a real belief in God which organized Christianity, as it is now, has so largely lost." He was awarded the Stalin Peace Prize in 1951.

Laski, Harold J. (1893–1950), one of the great theorists of the Fabian Society and the Labour Party, and professor of political science at the London School of Economics from 1926 until his death. Particularly in the 1930s, Laski was strongly influenced by Marxist theory, and saw socialism as the only alternative to fascism, but he wanted to adapt Marxism to Britain's liberal political tradition. He wrote many books, including *Reflections on the Revolution of Our Time*, which was self-consciously patterned after the *Reflections* of Edmund Burke, a man Laski admired. Laski was also deeply interested in the United States; as a young man he taught at Harvard and developed close friendships with Oliver Wendell Holmes, Louis Brandeis, and Felix Frankfurter. Many observers consider Laski's most interesting writing to be his correspondence with Holmes.

Strachey, John (1901–63) was son of the Conservative editor of *The Spectator,* but entered Parliament in 1929 as a follower of radical Labourite Sir Oswald Mosley. In 1931 he left the Labour Party with Mosley, but the two quickly diverged as Mosley became a fascist and Strachey a Communist in all but party affiliation. Throughout the thirties Strachey wrote a number of Marxist works, including *The Coming Struggle for Power* (1932) and *What Are We to Do?* (1938), intentionally modeled on Lenin's alarum. After the Soviet-Nazi collaboration, Strachey moved away from the Communists; he joined the first postwar Labour government as Food Minister, a post in which he gained a reputation for austerity, and later as War Minister. In 1939 he founded the Left Book Club with Laski and Victor Gollancz.

Tawney, Richard Henry (1880–1962) was an economic historian distinguished for his studies of Britain between 1540 and 1640 (known as Tawney's Century) and of preindustrial China, as well as for his controversial reworking of the Weber thesis in *Religion and the Rise of Capitalism* (1926). A professor at the London School of Economics, Tawney was active (as were other professors there) in Labour politics, and he contributed two of the most important works to the canon of British socialist theory: *The Acquisitive Society* (1920) and *Equality* (1931).

Wallas, Graham (1858–1932), a political psychologist, taught at the London School of Economics and was later University Professor of Political Science at the University of London. He joined the Fabian Society in 1886, shortly after George Bernard Shaw founded it, but Wallas resigned in 1904 because he disapproved of Fabian support for tariffs. Wallas's five books include *The Life of Francis Place, Human Nature in Politics,* and interestingly, *The Great Society* (1914).

Webb, Beatrice (1858–1943) and **Webb, Sidney James** (1859–1947), leaders of the Fabian Society, also founded *The New Statesman* and the London School of Economics and Political Science to help propagate and refine Fabian ideas. They were tireless researchers and wrote bulky histories of trade unionism and English local government, actually spending their 1892 honeymoon going through trade union records in Glasgow and Dublin. Sidney was active in the Labour Party, becoming President of the Board of Trade and Colonial Secretary; in 1929 he became Lord Passfield. Beatrice is celebrated for her *Minority Report* to the Royal Commission on the Poor, a paper that anticipated the Beveridge Report by thirty-five years. Until 1932 advocates of peaceful reform and of what they called "the inevitability of gradualness," the Webbs visited the Soviet Union that year and were sure they saw the future working. The question mark in the title of their 1935 book *Soviet Communism: A New Civilization?* was omitted from later editions.

—Prepared by the Editor

his bitter regret, socialism is often pictured as a state of affairs in which such "vocal socialists would feel thoroughly at home."

In parentheses it may be added that Orwell's own idea of "a state of affairs worth fighting for" is hardly more alluring. He found it in Barcelona during the Spanish Civil War: the wealthy classes apparently wiped out, the bourgeoisie killed or in flight, almost no "well-dressed" (his quotation marks) people, only rough working-class clothes, blue overalls, various military uniforms. . . . Here Orwell himself displays in an aberrant form that guilt-ridden mania for drabness and uniformity so characteristic of those he derides. And indeed, for all the vividness of his caricature of the intellectual, there is much that he could not see from the inside, so to speak. A prisoner cannot draw his prison without leaving his cell. Let us quote Orwell once more, and then step outside.

"The world, potentially at least," he cries elsewhere in *The Road to Wigan Pier,* "is immensely rich; develop it as it might be developed and we could all live like princes." Orwell here states, with more qualification than usual, a view common to nearly all intellectuals (see especially William Morris, who for Orwell was another dull windbag). Past and future progress are alike taken for granted. Yet past progress was the fruit of a system they despise and seek to end. How then can they be sure of future progress, or even of maintaining ground already conquered? How on earth would we know of these potential riches if capitalism had not thrust them under our noses? And these intellectuals often describe their mental processes as "scientific"! Does not science proceed with more prudence?

The typical intellectual is like the spoiled child of rich parents. He does not at first wonder why his parents and others are rich; this is for him the normal state of affairs. What bothers him, if he is at all curious, is why some should be poor. He does not see poverty and toil as the natural or original state of affairs, in which capitalism found nearly everybody and from which it has rescued many. No, it is poverty that has to be explained.

Our heir surveys the past and present coldly, without humility, wonder, or gratitude. He is not astonished that islands of wealth and culture should slowly and miraculously have risen from the sea of savagery, but vexed that civilization is not universal and evenly spread. In this respect he is what Tawney called an "intellectual villager," without background, terms of reference, or context. His vanity is often unbounded, typified by Shaw's amazing claim that he knew more about banking than any banker, a remark that reveals him to know even less about banking than the rest of us; contrast Goethe's profound humility in declaring that the invention of double-entry bookkeeping was one of the greatest achievements of the human mind.

Our heir becomes aware of and troubled by his own good fortune; he is often profoundly ignorant of his forebears' struggles, skills, services, and achievements, which are as incomprehensible to him as a watch to a monkey (Tawney's simile, sadly appropriate for his own contemptuous attitude to liberal civilization). Can it be that his forebears stole from the poor what was really theirs, that they enslaved, exploited, and disinherited them, milked them of surplus value? There are hundreds of books from Marx onward to tell him that this—part rubbish, part oversimplification—is so; and thus in self-righteous hatred, rage, and guilt he turns upon his parents and upon the capitalist system that they represent. (Strangely enough, we discern in this idea that the rich have robbed the poor of their birthright, a dim and unacknowledged survival of the golden-age myth, also discernible in Morris's medievalism and elsewhere.)

I have used the word "parents" half metaphorically. Yet

surely it is not fanciful to discern among so many British intellectuals an actual dislike, explicit or suppressed, of parents, children, and the family. H. G. Wells, for all too obvious reasons, directed the state to act as parent to all the children engendered by the free love he urged and practiced; and the catastrophist socialists, like the Communist poets of the thirties, urged the overthrow of existing society (including, by definition, of existing families) in the bizarre expectation that something better would emerge. But we also find a dislike for the family among those "moderate," reformist, egalitarian intellectuals like Mr. Crosland who strive, by savage taxation of income during life and of capital at death, as also by inflation, to deprive parents of one of their noblest incentives (another, the purchase of a decent education, Mr. Crosland seeks also to abolish). By such measures they deprive the old of dignity, the young of hope, and all families of the power to stay above mediocrity for more than one generation, and they illegitimate and repress a profound and valuable part of human nature, productive of much past progress.

I suspect that that Janus-faced mandarin Keynes in one of his many protean guises has done much to make such depredations respectable. It was he who said that in the long run we are all dead—a remark that would occur to few people with children of their own; he was more consistently egalitarian than he was consistently anything else; and he loudly proclaimed his contempt for the hereditary principle and for the control of wealth by "third-generation men." It is nonetheless odd that an intellectual so cultivated as Keynes should have preferred the first-generation climber to his third-generation successor, who usually has more leisure for thought, learning, art, patronage, and public work. Keynes publicly avowed his preference for the bourgeois "fish" against the proletarian "mud"; yet how on earth can any bourgeoisie arise if it is thrust back into the mud every time the bell tolls?

The intellectual justifies his attacks on hereditary culture by venomous caricatures of the attitudes and interests of the leisured and better-off classes. The American Thorstein Veblen's caricature is the most amusing, but it appears in forms more absurd and solemn in the jeremiads of his English forerunners, contemporaries, and disciples. The Webbs raved against the functionless rich, their futile occupations, licentious pleasures (including luring boys and girls into "concert rooms" for vice), and insolent manners; they were enraged by such gewgaws as the court, titles, soldiers, and diplomats; and they actually declared that "the very existence in any neighbourhood of a non-producing rich family, even if it is what it calls well-conducted, is by its evil example a blight on the whole district, lowering the standards, corrupting the morality and to that extent countering the work alike of the churches and the schools." These tirades, it should be added, were financed not only by domestic parsimony but also by Beatrice Webb's unearned annuity of £1,000 a year—a large sum in those days.

Shaw, himself a vast and greedy acquisitor, derided the pleasures of the rich—chocolates, cocktails, silly novels (what about silly plays?), motors, hotels. John Strachey (first a socialist, then a near-fascist, then a Stalinoid Marxist, then a Labour Minister, and rich throughout) denounced Macy's, Harrods, and the Galeries Lafayette, and hoped that privation would restore to the bourgeoisie their former power to think. The patrician Tawney sneered at the common vulgarity and bad manners of businessmen, though when shopgirls were rude he applauded. The moderate and hedonistic Mr. Crosland berates our "illiterate" wealthy classes for their cars and houses, holidays in Cannes, servants, gin(!), and other pleasures to most of which he is no stranger, and even for their failure to stop Georgian buildings from being knocked down. Who on earth does he think built them? And who is knocking them down? London University and local authorities are among the worst villains.

The extinction of such a philistine mob of loafers as is described above would be no loss. Envy is said to demand it, and would in Mr. Crosland's view be assuaged by its accomplishment. If the latter were true, the liquidation of the wealthier classes might arguably be desirable even if the poorer classes were, as I think inevitable, impoverished thereby. But Mr. Crosland and his friends grossly overestimate the present prevalence and virulence of envy (a misjudgment that may be explained by the fact that the only poorer people they know are sour Labour activists, notoriously hostile to everything in any way superior to themselves); they underestimate their own role in fostering and exploiting such envy as exists, thus, incidentally, making themselves objects of envy; they overlook the possibility that, in the relatively equal or "rationally" differentiated society they favor, envy would assume ever more vicious forms and find ever new victims for its malice; and, most important of all, they ignore the possibility that the suppression of envy may be essential to the survival of a free capitalist or "mixed" society and that its legitimization (or, by Tawney, virtual canonization) and subsequent triumph will be fatal alike to freedom and prosperity. (For a full treatment of this subject, see Helmut Schoek's brilliant book *Envy*.)

Now, if the civilized Mr. Crosland took any such threat seriously, he should be genuinely disturbed, for he has ceaselessly proclaimed his devotion to a mixed economy and a free society. What keeps him cheerful (if he still is, which we may doubt) is an almost unbounded optimism, akin to that felt by the classical economists (though far less securely reasoned) and far removed from the destructive and hysterical nihilism of the catastrophists. It expresses itself in a blind and irrational faith in the ability of capitalism somehow to deliver the goods, no matter how emasculated, overburdened, overregulated, diminished, and deprived alike of stick, carrot, confidence, hope, and rational motivation.

In *The Future of Socialism,* written in 1956, Mr. Crosland declared that full employment could be easily achieved and maintained by judicious and timely expansion of domestic demand, that is, by that "continuing mild inflation" that he and other moderates consider tolerable or even beneficial. He ignored the likelihood that inflation, in order to perform the beneficent task he allotted to it, must be less and less mild, more and more rapid and progressive, always a bit more than is expected; for "expected" inflation is discounted in advance and produces no effect on demand. Hence in part our present difficulties, with an unprecedented inflation rate and rising unemployment.

In the same book Mr. Crosland regarded further rapid growth as both essential and certain; no need to bother about it, it can be taken for granted. If it goes on, as it will, material poverty will cease to be a problem. Other problems will indeed remain, fortunately for intellectuals whose lives would be empty without them; not only problems of resentment and envy caused by residual inequalities, but also other problems in the fields of psychology, sociology, divorce reform, and so forth. But economics as the dismal science will have served its turn; prosperity is here to stay; investment incentives will remain buoyant, with high savings, high incomes, and high consumption; adequate capital formation is assured, risks of depreciation much reduced. "We stand in Britain," Mr. Crosland excitedly proclaimed in 1956, "on the threshold of mass abundance." Hey-ho.

"The enjoyment of personal success," Professor Hayek has written, "will be given to large numbers only in a society that, as a whole, progresses fairly rapidly," and in

which as a consequence more people are rising than falling
—and in which indeed most of those falling are falling only
relatively though still rising absolutely. It was to such a fortunate society that Mr. Crosland confidently looked forward; and, had his expectations been fulfilled, it is probable
that the nit-picking envies and resentments that elsewhere
obsess him would fade into insignificance, affording little
material for distress or further exploitation.

But alas, at least for the time being, things have turned
out very differently. We in Britain find ourselves in a sta-
tionary or declining state of society, the former described
by Adam Smith as "hard" and "dull" for rich and poor
alike, the latter "miserable" and "melancholy." In such
states class hatred and bitterness must thrive, together with
those who cause, exacerbate, and exploit our miseries. How
has this come to pass?

The most important clue lies in Mr. Crosland's extraordinary views about economic incentive and motivation,
views that are fully shared not only by other intellectuals
but also by successive Labour governments (to which he
has been intellectual-in-residence) and their more responsible supporters, and that have clearly guided or justified
policy.

"We know too little about incentives," concedes Mr.
Crosland at one point, "to make firm statements"—firm
statements about whether "equality and rapid growth are
hard to reconcile" and about whether "socialist policies
must necessarily slow down the rate of growth." Such doubts
would induce in other, more modest men, if they valued
growth as he does, an extreme caution in enforcing equality, in destroying existing incentives, and in pressing ahead
with socialist policies. Not so with Mr. Crosland.

Everywhere in his writings he derides the contribution of
financial incentive, competition, profit, and individualism
to economic growth; technological and productive ad-

vances, in his view, spring rather from "people working on a fixed salary in a large managerial structure." He urges that, if anything, this fixed salary should be lowered, by taxation or other means, for he believes that the spread of income in Britain, though narrower than in the Soviet Union (a country he oddly supposes to be egalitarian), is far too wide. And he thinks that the rewards for saving and investment are far too high, and may be safely reduced.

Mr. Crosland conceded in 1956 that "some danger point must evidently exist at which equality begins to react really seriously on the supply of ability (and also of effort, risk-taking, and so on), and hence on economic growth. Where exactly this point lies, no one knows. I do not myself believe we have yet reached it."

Implicit in these remarks is the odd assumption that, once the danger point is reached, we can somehow retrace our steps to safer ground and all will be well again. Yet despite their ignorance of where the danger point lies, or of what to do when they get there, the practice of Mr. Crosland and his friends has been to press ruthlessly on till even they see unmistakable signs that it has been reached. With irresponsible levity they proceed on their mad experiment, like some ignorant peasant cheerfully piling more and more onto a half-starved donkey, or some crazy doctor in a concentration camp using prisoners to find out how much cold the human body can stand.

Without intending it, they may do grave and irreparable damage, and may have already done it; indeed, they might have done it even before Crosland wrote, for, already some twenty years before he wrote, Evan Durbin, one of the most civilized and percipient of intellectuals, had lamented that taxation was too high to permit the continued vigorous survival of the free economy. It was for this reason that Durbin had become a reluctant but convinced socialist.

What are the signs that the danger point has now been

reached? With their general contempt for economic motivation, Mr. Crosland and his friends are not likely to be the
first to see them. Indeed, like Laski (and like Graham
Wallas, who considered, perhaps playfully, that even ab-
normally strong acquisitive instincts might in the future express themselves in the collection of shells or postage
stamps) they prefer to rely on other sorts of motivation to
keep the show on the road—the self-identification of business leaders with their firms, professional pride, desire for
prestige, public esteem, and greed for power. Why these
motives should be preferred is not always clear. Greed for
power is not usually regarded as an attractive quality, and
Dr. Johnson thought no man so innocently employed as in
making money. "Prestige" is often only a pretty word for
pompous public relations, for hobnobbing with politicians,
in Britain for a hunt for titles, and for conspicuous waste in
general.

Nor are all the signs of that danger point particularly
easy to spot or quantify. How on earth can one measure
such impalpables as effort withheld, enterprise thwarted,
hopes blasted, skills unacquired or wasted, idleness preferred? The resultant torpor is not even spread uniformly
through the economy; incentives totally inadequate at one
point may still elicit effort elsewhere. National economic
failure is of course measurable in many ways; we are getting expert at it. But Mr. Crosland is still entitled to debate
to what extent measurable failure is due to lack of incentive.

Less debatable, more measurable, and perhaps less re-
versible is the rising tide of skilled and talented émigrés
that I expect will soon become torrential, an exodus that
will leave behind a stagnant and impoverished quagmire
bereft alike of wealth and culture. But when this exodus becomes apparent to all, it will be too late to stanch the flow;
nor will those who have already gone be drawn back by

sudden changes of heart or policy in a socialist party that they have grown to mistrust, fear, and hate, that is generally hostile to their interests, and that can never be permanently excluded from office.

Mr. Crosland is still patiently watching the dials, but he does not seem to see what we see: a nation bleeding to death. Nor is this wholly surprising, for in fact one can learn more about human motivations and frustrations, about intentions and despair, by talking to ordinary people in a pub than by poring over the official statistics and surveys that are the intellectual's normal source of information.

Now the present shambles in Britain does not bear much resemblance to the ordered Utopias envisaged by intellectuals like the Webbs, Laski, and Tawney. Yet, if our country is (relatively) poorer, less free, more equal, and less competitive than it was, it is probable that the teachings of such intellectuals have powerfully contributed to these developments, laudable or deplorable as different people may think them.

The Webbs and Laski certainly expected vast material wealth to be produced by the elimination of capitalist "waste" and "inefficiency." They might indeed be disappointed by the results of progress so far achieved, but I presume they would still advise us to press on. Tawney cared less about material wealth than vague spiritual assets like fellowship, and would be distressed less by our drabness than by our morose ill humor and by the class hatred that declining fortune always exacerbates.

But I think all four would kick up a hullabaloo where I have said "less free." "Less free for whom?" they would cry, for like most intellectuals, they muddle the difference between the *freedom* to do something and the *power* to do it. Without power, freedom to them is a mere useless formality, a hollow mockery, like the beggar's freedom to enter the Ritz. Freedom that is enjoyed only by a minority is not to them freedom at all, but a privilege at best to be tolerated, more likely obliterated.

An equal society is thus by definition to them a free society, in which no freedoms exist (or *need* exist) that all do not have the power to enjoy, and in which all can enjoy such freedoms as may exist, if any, and thus be "free." A society of slaves might thus be a free society in their eyes; indeed, I am sure that this philosophical confusion—as well as ignorance, gullibility, callous indifference to suffering, and that hypertrophied sense of order to which Orwell referred—helps to explain the scandalous prostration of British intellectuals before the full horrors of Stalin's tyranny in the thirties and forties. Among those who abased themselves were the Webbs, Laski, John Strachey, Stephen Spender, the Red Dean Hewlett Johnson, and many others, all listed in David Caute's book *The Fellow Travellers*. In some of these cases a harsher term than callous indifference is appropriate, for who does not know, and cannot find in the literature of the thirties if he looks, that positive delight in cruelty and violence from which book-learned ideologues have never been immune?

Beatrice Webb herself wondered why British socialists should be more sympathetic than their Continental counterparts to Russian Communism. I suspect the reason may lie not only in greater ignorance, but also in the complacency bred by distance and by the reassuring presence of the English Channel and the Royal Navy, at that time still formidable; for the Webbs at least were actually timid petty bourgeois, highly respectful of "established expectations" (including their own annuity) and terrified of revolution, which their own inevitable gradualness seems largely designed to avert. Their conversion to Communism, on the face of it incongruous, took place only when disorder had been ferociously suppressed in the Soviet Union and when the risk of disorder in the West, thanks to the Depression, seemed imminent. What they worshiped was always power and success.

People like the Webbs, unable to tell the difference between freedom and power, are obviously very inadequate defenders of freedom, if not actually hostile to it. At best they are coarsely indifferent, at worst harshly inimical, to minority tastes, cultural interests, and moral beliefs, and also to the freedoms that protect them. And in general such intellectuals are totally unable to see the ways in which we all benefit by freedoms that only some of us can enjoy. We may well lack the means or the brains to write the equivalent of Shaw's plays, say, or the Webbs' vast *oeuvre*; but I do not think Shaw or the Webbs are in a good position to deny that we may have benefited from them. Few people could make use of the artistic freedom in Tsarist Russia, and the Webbs would therefore regard that freedom as formal and valueless. Yet the use Tolstoy and Dostoievsky made of their freedom has enriched the lives of millions who lacked the power and now lack the freedom to express themselves fully.

In the same way, Tawney somewhere blandly describes competition as being of value only to those able to compete. What rubbish this is! I do not myself have to be able to compete in order to profit by the competition of rival playwrights, biscuit makers, ideologues, and doctors for my patronage; indeed, as *tertius gaudens,* I profit more obviously than those who compete and fail and may be ruined by their efforts.

Another piece of Tawney nonsense, while we are at it, expresses the moral hatred that he and fellow intellectuals feel for capitalist society. How can people live for service and self-sacrifice, he wails, if society is dominated by ruthless egotism? Why can they not? One may question whether capitalist society is more or less dominated by ruthless egotism than other societies. What cannot so easily be doubted is the freedom it confers on all to live lives of service and self-sacrifice if they so wish. The great classical economists did not say that people *should* be dominated by ruthless egotism. They described men as they are, governed among other motives by an egotism, whether ruthless or enlightened, that may by freedom and wise regulation be turned to public good. If the good life could be lived under Nero, why on earth not under Gladstone?

I described our society today as "less competitive," and here too I think our intellectuals would demur. For one thread running through all their works is that competition, whether desirable or not (it is usually qualified by such epithets as "disorderly," "wasteful," "cutthroat," "unregulated," and so forth), was by the time they wrote dying or dead, being succeeded everywhere by the monopoly that Marx predicted.

Three considerations, to my mind, they entirely overlooked. Baldly stated, without qualifications otherwise desirable, one is that there is no natural or theoretic tendency toward monopoly in an unregulated capitalist system. Another is that those parts of the British and American economies that are monopolistically controlled have not grown much in the past seventy years—except where, in Britain, the government has intervened vigorously either to promote private concentration (as in the thirties) or, as it has done since 1945, to promote monopolistic public corporations. The third is that monopolies should, as Joseph Schumpeter advised, be regarded not only as they are *now*, or at some other particular moment, but also *in time*. What looks like as unassailable monopoly is in fact (unless protected by statute—a very important exception) a fragile structure, its shaky foundations forever washed and eroded by the currents of competition that surge whenever technical advance and new needs make them possible and desira-

ble. For these reasons the wise monopolist is not like the intellectual's caricature of him: he is a timid, not an arrogant
man, always behaving as though he were not a monopolist
at all. He knows that his position, formidable as it looks to
the thoughtless, is in fact constantly menaced by the irresistible forces of modern technological "creative destruc-
tion" (Schumpeter's phrase for what the Webbs call
"waste").

Thus for the Webbs and their friends there arose no
question of preserving or extending competition, which was
deservedly moribund. Their task was to devise another and
quite different industrial system that would do all that competition had ever done, but more and better. This was the
purpose of their vast and all-embracing Babel tower of national and local and municipal boards and public corporations, producing all goods and supplying all services, not
for profit but to satisfy measured and objective needs
(rather than "appetites"—for some reason a dirty word for
them) and to fulfill a majestic public purpose.

It would be quite unjust to accuse them of seeking to impose upon us a uniform tyranny. They wanted to maintain
a variety of goods and services (provided profits were excluded), and the whole structure was to be democratically
controlled through numberless channels by the "organized"
and "informed" criticism of consumers. Yet somehow we
doubt their democratic protestations. We note their raptur-
ous submission to the Soviet Union, which forcibly suggests
that their devotion to the machinery was far greater than to
the democratic spirit that was supposed to inform it. We
also note tones of voice, turns of phrase, and manners of
speech. Beatrice Webb regarded elections as a device to get
the "conscious consent" of the governed. Local government
is for Laski merely "educative"—that is, the citizens are
there to be instructed, not to control their so-called servants. He quotes with approval Sir Arthur Salter's pompous

dictum that "committees are an invaluable instrument for breaking administrative measures onto the back of the public." And Laski is everywhere vexed and alarmed by the possibility that socialist plans might be reversed "by some chance hazard of electoral fortune." At one stage he therefore thought it proper to demand of the Tories, as a condition of their return to office, a pledge that they would repeal no socialist measures.

Nowhere here can we find any genuine respect for democracy. Moreover, throughout the outpourings of all these intellectuals runs an obsession with war and the supposed achievements of arbitrary wartime governments, with their direction of labor, capital, and materials—an obsession particularly ludicrous in people so ovine and unwarlike, and an obsession certainly inimical to democracy and freedom. We find over and over again, particularly in the work of Sir William Beveridge, a socialist in all but name, the view that freedom is a peacetime luxury that we can no longer afford even in peacetime, in which as in war the economy must be directed by what he typically describes as an economic general staff. Those who have actually served in any kind of armed forces are normally less respectful of the extreme efficiency of military methods.

Tawney is more of a democrat, but a peculiarly hectoring one. He is forever demanding that citizens *must* "participate" in committees and industrial boards and local governments and so forth; he considers it not merely a right but also a duty incumbent on us all to be "concerned, self-educated and active." This is a false conception of liberty, a gross invasion of the right to privacy, which indeed is always one of the goods to be "socialized"—that is, destroyed.

Why on earth should we "participate" in all these activities, to many of us profoundly tedious? Why should Evelyn Waugh, say, or Stravinsky (or even Tawney himself, did he not wish to) bother himself about municipal buses, bakeries, housing, and sewage? We may not think ourselves qualified to meddle with such matters. We may not wish to obtain the qualifications. We may think we have more important things to do, a concept presumably incomprehensible to Tawney, who defined citizenship for the scholar as "knowledge applied to social improvement." No classical scholar, for instance, could by this definition be a citizen.

Yet indeed with the establishment of all the institutions proposed by people like the Webbs, Laski, and Tawney, it might seem to the rest of us at once impossible *and* desperately important to participate in all of them, to prevent them from being dominated by people like the Webbs, Laski, and Tawney, and by all the hordes of qualified scientific socialist experts favored by them, to whom of course these institutions would be infinitely congenial. There would exist what was described by Orwell, quoted above: "a state of affairs in which such vocal socialists would feel thoroughly at home"—yes, indeed, and they alone; for the rest of us would be excluded, by our own decision if not by that of the vocal socialists themselves.

To the vast extent that our economy has been removed from the private to the public sector, we already suffer from a stagnant tyranny of busybodies and bureaucrats. This again was not the Webbs' ideal. One motive force in particular is missing, and that is the supposedly tremendous power of organized consumer criticism to maintain and increase efficiency and to ensure that new processes are promptly introduced and new needs met. Pitiful organs to this end do exist in the ineffective representation of "consumers" on national boards and in Parliament, which is, of course, as the Webbs recognized, totally incapable of controlling the vast and complex functions that it has arrogated to itself. But the Webbs' vast machinery at present

Commissioner Mark is fully aware of these problems and determined to deal with them squarely. He is just as determined, however, to confront what he takes to be the deficiencies in the rest of the criminal justice system. He is unsparing in his criticism of lawyers and judges, the former for obstructing the search for the truth, the latter for allowing the guilty to go unpunished. For years, in a way unthinkable for most politically cautious (because politically vulnerable) American police chiefs—Edward Davis of Los Angeles being a conspicuous exception—Mark has pressed for revisions in the laws of criminal procedure. He was among those who, in 1967, objected to the ability of a lone juror to prevent the conviction of a guilty man. The response was a law (presented by a Labour Party minister!) that allowed for convictions by a less-than-unanimous jury, in general by ten out of the twelve (the actual formula is much more complex). By the same law, the Criminal Justice Act of 1967, the defense was required to disclose before the trial any alibi the accused planned to offer so that the police might investigate it (the entirety of the prosecution's case must be disclosed in advance).

Now Commissioner Mark and others are pressing for additional changes. He would like to waive the need for a police caution—that familiar phrase by which the arrested party is warned that what he says can be used in evidence against him (in the United States, it is known as the "Miranda warning"). As Mark puts it, "the credibility of the accused should be related to his spontaneity rather than to that period of reflection and professional consultation between his original interrogation and trial, a period which has produced . . . some of the most ingenious and highly paid fiction of our time." He would also like to weaken the right not to testify in one's own trial, at least by allowing the prosecution to put the accused in the witness box, ask him questions, and call to the jury's attention any refusal to answer.[29]

lacks the powerful motor and controls they thus devised for it. Would it not go better if consumer wants could be made known?

How could they be? The Webbs envisaged that you and I, or they (it matters not) should collectively as consumers make known what we want and make sure that we get it. At the moment we do this without fuss or palaver, by buying this but not that, by shopping not here but there. Is it seriously suggested that we should turn up in endless tedious committees to argue our preference for New Zealand butter and French burgundy over French butter and Australian burgundy? Perhaps not; more sensible to delegate our choice to some elected manager. But he is only answerable to us as a *mass*. He need not bother about individual or minority preferences; he is not bound to us by the nexus of profit and loss; if he pleases ten, he can afford to ignore nine with impunity.

But so far we deal only with existing wants and known preferences. When we get on to new processes for satisfying existing wants, the difficulties multiply; how am I to know of such processes? Experts may advise me, but experts are notoriously indifferent to considerations of cost; like the Webbs themselves, they tend to prefer the best *technically* to the best *economically,* and to exaggerate the importance of maximum output irrespective of cost.

And when we get on to new wants, what we don't yet want but shall want when we see it, the difficulties multiply at a compound rate. How can I be concerned or active about what I cannot envisage? How can I expect committees and experts to be concerned and active on my behalf? Why should they be? Their life is easier if novelty is suppressed, and no more profitable if it is not.

Like other intellectuals, the Webbs, Laski, and the rest seem wholly incapable of grasping the role of risk-taking and profit- or loss-making in the maintenance of economic efficiency and above all in innovation. If they could have grasped it, they would never have proposed to substitute for it, magically simple and infinitely complex as it is, their foothills and mountain ranges of boards and committees, their swarming hives of bureaucrats and busybodies and experts, their snowstorms of paper, their echoing wastes of gassing and boredom, their pandemonium of ceaseless but sterile controversy.

"We find," wrote de Tocqueville, "an administration almost as numerous as the population, preponderant, interfering, regulating, restricting, insisting upon foreseeing everything, controlling everything, and understanding the interests of those under its control better than they do themselves; in short, in a constant state of barren activity. . . ."

He was writing of French Canada under the *ancien régime.* He might have been writing either of the Webbs' Utopia or of Britain today. In St. Paul's Cathedral, you many find Sir Christopher Wren's tremendous epitaph: *"Si monumentum requiris, circumspice"* (If you seek his monument, look around you). If you seek the Webbs' monument, come to Britain today.

Crime and Punishment in England

James Q. Wilson

However much Americans may deplore the apparent political and economic decay of England, there persists among nearly all of us the admiring view that at least with respect to criminal justice, the English know how to do things properly. The images about British justice with which we have been supplied by countless reporters and storytellers remain unsullied and intact—the quiet, competent, incorruptible bobby; the stern but fair judge; the quick and certain punishment for wrongdoers; the respect and deference shown by all ranks of the English population toward unarmed constables; the safety and security of the meanest streets of London. To be sure, we are aware of some incidents of terrorist violence and an occasional football riot, but surely these are isolated and modest exceptions to the normal state of affairs.

This view of English crime and justice follows naturally upon a more general perception of British society widely taught and believed in the United States. There is thought to be in Britain a broad consensus in moral and legal matters —no competing value systems either generate crime or stimulate disrespect for the law. To these common habits of mind is joined a pragmatic disposition to devise rational and useful schemes for insuring both private rights and public safety—careful, formal trials for anybody accused of a crime, prompt and severe sentences for anybody convicted of one. What we perceive, in short, is a legal system codified by Blackstone and supported by a sentencing policy devised by Bentham, all operating in a society described by Bagehot.

It would make a fine literary effect if I could at this point show that the very opposite of these suppositions is in fact the case. The reality of British justice, however, while quite different from what is popularly imagined, is by no means the exact reverse of its image. The current state of criminal justice in England and Wales is enormously complex, in part because it is almost as diverse and lacking in central direction as its American counterpart, in part because it is the object of a strenuous debate over its purposes and practices, and in part because it is struggling, inadequately, to cope with a level of crime undreamed of as recently as twenty years ago. What can be said is that were the economic crisis of the country not uppermost in the minds of everyone, the problem of crime might well be; by the same token, were the government in a position to increase expenditures on anything (which it very nearly is not), it might arguably give highest priority to the expansion and improvement of the police and the prisons.

It is clear that the current economic and political crisis powerfully affects the prospects for any bold action to deal with crime. What is not clear is whether that crisis—or rather the change in society and popular attitudes that have contributed to that crisis—has itself been a cause of the steep increase in crime that has occurred in recent years. It is clear that the political economy of England has come very near to collapse; whether the civic virtue of its people is in an equally perilous state and, if so, whether from the same causes, is not at all clear.

What can be said is this: England and Wales are in the

grip of the most steeply rising crime rate of this century. This crime wave has stretched the police service and the capacity of the prison system almost to the breaking point. Accompanying (and perhaps contributing to) the crime increase have been changes in the criminal justice system that have substantially lessened the probability that any given offender will be penalized or separated from the rest of society, and this is especially true of young offenders. While certain cases are still dealt with swiftly, this is generally true only for less important ones or (not necessarily the same thing) ones in which the likely penalty is trivial. The congestion and delay in the disposition of serious cases has increased dramatically. Finally, there are signs of what I would call, at the obvious risk of some transatlantic ill will, the Americanization of English criminal justice, by which I mean that well-intentioned officials and advisers in Her Majesty's government seem to have learned little from the mistakes made by similarly situated persons in the United States. There is scarcely a single ill-advised recommendation of the President's Commission on Law Enforcement and Administration of Justice that the British Home Office and its various advisory councils do not seem determined to repeat.

CRIME AND ITS "CAUSES"

It is widely believed that in the United States the crime rate is vastly—incomparably—larger than it is in England. Indeed, even if the comparison is restricted to the largest cities, the differences are supposedly enormous—London is claimed to have only a small fraction of the crime reported in New York. In fact, comparing all "serious" offenses ("indictable offenses" in England and "index crimes" in the United States), the United States has more, but not vastly more, than England. In 1973, there were 4,116 "index crimes" per 100,000 population reported to the police in the United States, and 2,760 "indictable offenses" per 100,000 reported in England and Wales. The London Metropolitan Police (which excludes the City of London) reported 355,248 indictable offenses in 1973; the New York City Police Department reported 475,855 index crimes the same year. The populations of the two cities are approximately the same.[1]

"Index crimes" and "indictable offenses" are not exactly the same thing, and in consequence some may feel that any gross comparison of English and American crime figures is misleading. To a degree, that is true. But consider one or two specific crimes that are more or less commonly defined and commonly counted. There were 1,211 burglaries for every 100,000 persons in the United States in 1973; there were 800 burglaries for every 100,000 persons in England and Wales that year—a difference, to be sure, but not one so vast as is often supposed. And if one were to adjust the English and American figures for the differences in the availability of things worth stealing—color television sets, ten-speed bicycles, fancy camera gear—the burglary rate in England might well appear even higher than is reported.

Another objection to the English/American comparison is that we are dealing only with *reported* offenses. We know, of course, that many offenses go unreported. It is possible that citizens report to the police a higher proportion of all burglaries in England than in the United States. Until the results of a British survey of criminal victimization are published, we will not know. But in the meantime, we can examine the rates for one crime—auto theft—that we know from surveys to be quite accurately reported in this country, and that we need not believe is any less completely reported in England. By my calculations, in England and Wales there were 2,056 motor vehicles stolen out of every 100,000 owned by households in 1973, a theft rate *twice as great* as in the United States, where there were just over 1,000 stolen automobiles for every 100,000 registered.

Nor are English thefts petty. F. H. McClintock and N. Howard Avison estimate that the average value of the property stolen per burglary or larceny in 1965 was in excess of $100 (now it is no doubt more), and they note that the greatest increases in theft have occurred in the category of high-loss crimes.[2]

There *are* major differences in English and American crime rates, but they are primarily with respect to violent crimes. In 1973, 1,680 murders were reported to the New York City Police Department, but only 110 were reported to the London Metropolitan Police. The total of 72,750 robberies reported in New York was nearly twenty-seven times greater than the 2,680 robberies reported in London. Londoners may be only a little less dishonest than New Yorkers, but they are vastly less violent.

England, including London, has experienced a great increase in the rate of reported serious (that is, "indictable") offenses, but the increase in certain violent offenses, notably robbery, has been even greater. In 1955, there were only 823 robberies in all of England and Wales; in 1974, there were 8,666. This was a tenfold increase in number and, since the population did not grow much during this period, nearly a tenfold increase in rate. The rise has been even greater in London: There were 237 robberies reported there in 1955 but 3,151 in 1974, a thirteenfold increase. As a result, a larger percentage of all thefts are now accompanied by violence than was the case ten or twenty years ago. In 1955, Colin Greenwood reports, less than .3 per cent of all London thefts were robberies; by 1969, it was nearly 1 per cent, and it continues to grow. (In comparison, about 17 per cent of all New York thefts are robberies.)[3]

The very great restrictions placed by English law on the private possession of firearms have not apparently impeded the increase in robbery. Blunt and sharp instruments —pick handles and knives, primarily—continue to be the favored weapon in armed robberies, accounting for over half of them. The number of robberies in which guns were used or carried has also increased greatly. Colin Greenwood concludes that there has been a steady increase in the use of violence in the commission of theft, that the number of robberies in which weapons were used has increased at least as fast as the number of robberies, and that there has been a sharp rise in the proportion of armed robberies in which the weapon available was a firearm.[4] Despite legal restrictions, the steady shift from unarmed to armed robbery has proceeded apace; where there is a will, there is a way.

Though the trends are ominous, London has a long way to go before violence there approximates violence in New York (or most other large American cities). What accounts for this great difference could occupy a speculative mind for years. I am aware of no scientific or systematic evidence that would shed light on it. One possibility will occur immediately to an American reader: the differences in the composition of the population or, to be blunt, race.

Certainly if you were to ask a taxi driver, hotel clerk, or news vendor in London, they would explain the increase in violent crime, especially robbery, by the presence of West Indians. The Americans term for robbery of the person on a street following a sudden attack—"mugging"—has caught the fancy of the English, and one finds frequent reference to it in the press, even though it lacks any precise legal definition. There is no doubt that muggings have increased in London—from 674 in 1968 to 1,544 in 1972, according to the police.[5] The total is still, by American standards, ridiculously small—the prospect of four or five

muggings a day in a city of 8 million persons is not likely to
inspire fear in the heart of a Manhattanite. It is widely
believed that these muggings are the work of black youths,
but it is impossible to verify this. Though the Metropolitan
Police—Scotland Yard—records the race of those whom it
arrests, it will not divulge the data, nor will the Home
Office, to which the police commissioner reports. A confi-
dential study on race and crime was in fact made by the statistical unit of Scotland Yard, but the results are closely
guarded.

Map displays of robberies and other violent crimes, however, show that these crimes are common in the heavily
West Indian sections of London, such as Lambeth and
Brixton, and on or near London Underground (subway)
lines that serve those and similar areas. The authorities refuse to publish data on these matters, fearing that such
facts would be exploited by anti-immigrant politicians and
would unduly inflame popular prejudices. (Presumably the
government would release the data if they would tend to
soothe popular fears.)

Whatever may be the relationship between race and violent crime, immigrants cannot by any stretch of the imagination account for more than a small fraction of the total
increase of crime in England. The rate at which indictable
offenses are committed began rising in about 1930, quadru-
pling in the two decades before 1950. There was a pause
just after World War II, with a few years of declining crime
rates, and then an even more rapid surge began in 1955
that has continued, with brief respite in 1972–73, to the
present.[6] Crime has increased during the past two decades
at a rate of about 10 per cent per year (about the same as
the rate of increase in the United States). Though immigra-
tion to England was also increasing during this period (the
number of persons living in Great Britain who were born
overseas doubled between 1951 and 1971), the fraction of

the total population born abroad has been quite small—3.2 per cent in 1951, 5.5 per cent in 1971. (The British census does not report the number of persons born in Britain of foreign or mixed parentage.)[7]

Furthermore, most immigrants are either not "colored" (they are from Canada, Australia, New Zealand, Ireland), or are Asians (Indians and Pakistanis) whom every observer believes have lower than average crime rates. The proportion of persons living in England born in the West Indies is very small indeed—less than 2 per cent for Britain as a whole, and slightly more than 2 per cent for London.[8] Finally, McClintock and Avison, studying criminal repeaters, found that well over 80 per cent of the known recidivists were born in England or Wales.[9]

What, then, can account for the great increase in English crime rates? There is no agreed-upon answer to that question, nor is there likely to be one. It is instructive for Americans to contemplate the problem, however, because the increase in English crime, in many ways so similar to the increase in the United States, cannot be explained by the various "causes" regularly advanced in this country. Race, as we have seen, may explain some of the increase in violent crime, but it cannot explain much of the increase in crime generally. Nor can the increased youthfulness of the population account for much of the change. The number of boys under the age of seventeen increased between 1961 and 1971 by 8 per cent in Britain and 9 per cent in the United States—a contribution to the rising crime rate, no doubt, but scarcely the decisive one.[10] In England as in the United States, it is not simply or even primarily the growth in the *numbers* of young persons but rather the increased rate of crime *among* young persons that has caused crime rates to rise. Put in technical terms, the age-specific crime rate has increased, most notably among the younger age groups. For example, in 1951 only 1,164 out of every

100,000 males between the ages of seventeen and twenty-one were convicted of an indictable offense in England and Wales. By 1973, that had quintupled: Now 5,522 out of every 100,000 males in that age group were found guilty. (The conviction rate for persons over thirty increased only slightly.)[11]

Trying to explain the increased criminality of the young in England is as frustrating as trying to explain it in the United States. Narcotics addiction, which may explain some part of American crime rates, cannot explain more than a tiny fraction in England, where there are very few addicts (though the few who exist are quite likely to have criminal records despite the availability of heroin from government clinics). Nor can the rising crime rate in England be accounted for by rising unemployment, increased income inequality, or deepening poverty. In 1961, the unemployment rate in Great Britain was 1.4 per cent; in 1973, it was 2.7 per cent. During the years in which crime was rising the fastest, unemployment was virtually nonexistent; the two recent years (1971 and 1972) in which unemployment exceeded 3 per cent were the years in which, for the only time in the past two decades, the crime rate actually went down.[12]

So also with income inequality. The government reports that there has been a steady decline since at least 1961, and probably earlier, in the proportion of the national wealth owned by the richest tenth of the population and a corresponding increase in the proportion owned by the least wealthy tenth.[13] Being aware of these facts, no one in England tries to explain crime rate changes by the pauperization of the workers, though most recognize that crime is more common among *certain kinds* of lower-income families.

What kinds? The association between crime and aspects of family life, repeatedly established in America, has also been shown to operate in England, beginning with the pioneering study by Sir Cyril Burt in 1925 of young delinquents in London and continuing with Professor Sprott's 1954 study of delinquent and nondelinquent areas in a working-class mining town.[14] The familial contribution to English crime does not, however, depend on whether the family is "broken"—that is, whether one parent is absent owing to divorce or desertion—or on whether the mother is working. Absent or working parents are no more likely to have delinquent children than intact, at-home families; it is the *behavior* of the parents that is crucial. Discord, the absence of affection and consistent discipline, and improper moral instruction are the causal factors; on this, the studies of Lee Robins, Barbara Wootton, Simon Yudkin, Harriet Wilson, and John Mays all seem to agree.[15]

That it is the behavior rather than the number of parents that accounts for delinquency helps explain why youthful crime can increase in England though there has been no increase in the proportion of single-parent families (they accounted for less than 7 per cent of all households in both 1961 and 1971).[16] What we would like to measure, but obviously cannot, is the change that has occurred in the quality of family life in the past two decades. Though it may pain the sophisticated eye to encounter such apparently Victorian statements, it seems inescapable that we have witnessed a change in the moral quality of family life that has had, along with other factors, a profound effect on the general level of public safety and security.

What these other factors may be is largely a matter of conjecture. What is striking—and, given the tendencies of American thought, salutary—is the absence in England of the kinds of conjectures heard in the United States. Neither the authorities nor the scholars in Britain "explain" rising crime by reference to poverty, drug abuse, relative deprivation, social or political frustration, rising unemployment, or the absence of legitimate opportunities. Such factors simply cannot account for the crime increase in England; one suspects they cannot account for it in the United States either, but that our parochial perspective has prevented us from seeing that.

Crime is rising in virtually every society for which reliable data are available. Though it is possible that different causes are at work in different countries, it is also possible— and, given the similarity in the trends, more than likely— that some general factors are operating on a worldwide scale. Three immediately come to mind: the growth of urbanization and affluence; the spread, especially among the young, of the cult of personal liberation and unfettered self-expression; and the change in attitudes of the young toward authority, schooling, and the family. There is no way of testing the effect of the subjective forces, but there is some evidence on the importance of the objective ones; for example, in England as in America, the rise in thefts of automobiles is, as Leslie Wilkins has shown, closely related to the rise in the number of registered motor vehicles. The more opportunities for theft, the more thefts will be committed, other things being equal.[17]

THE POLICE AND CRIME

One of the things that may not be equal is the risk associated with crime, and two of the factors that may influence that are the number and efficiency of the police. In theory, the English police are locally controlled organizations that might, were the theory fact, have as great difficulty in adjusting their jurisdiction, resources, and training to changing criminal conditions as have their American counterparts. In reality, there is a sizable degree of national control, financing, and standardization of the police service. Half the cost of each local force is paid for out of national funds disbursed by the Home Office. Regulations governing almost every feature of police service are promulgated by the Home Secretary, and Her Majesty's inspector of the constabulary carries out detailed reviews to insure that these regulations are obeyed by every local force. There is a single Police College, at Bramshill, through which virtually all of the up-and-coming senior officers have passed or will pass on their way to command positions in the various local forces. Each prospective chief constable is expected to have served in at least one other jurisdiction before he is appointed to head a local force. One dramatic measure of the degree of national control is the fact that within the past decade, the number of local police forces has been reduced from 125 to 43. A comparable reduction—by two thirds!—in the number of American police departments is simply unthinkable.

These consolidations, regulations, and training schemes are aimed at improving police efficiency. They are not, however, accompanied by equally significant increases in money or manpower. Metropolitan London, with a population of about 8 million, has only 21,000 police officers (New York City has a third again as many); London has about the same number of police today as it did forty years ago, when crime was only a fourth as common.

The failure of police forces to expand during a period of increasing crime and greater public disorder has been accompanied by a sharp drop in the proportion of reported offenses cleared by an arrest or confession. Between 1938 and 1954, a period when crime rates were more or less stable, the "detection rate" (that is, the proportion of all reported crimes that the police believe they have "cleared up") was between 40 and 50 per cent. As the crime rate began going up in 1955, the detection rate began going down. From 1955 to 1965, according to McClintock and Avison, it dropped by 10 per cent.[18] This rate has continued to drop down to the present, and is lowest in the biggest cities.

There are grave difficulties in relying too heavily on "detection rates" as a measure of police efficiency, or indeed as a measure of anything. The number does not discriminate between serious and trivial offenses, between crimes solved by arresting a hitherto unknown suspect and crimes admitted to by a person already in custody, and between crimes (such as burglary) that typically require police action for their solution and crimes (such as drug abuse) that are known of only because an arrest has already been made. Nevertheless, there seems little doubt that the chances of any given offender being caught for a crime today are substantially less than they would have been for a crime ten or twenty years ago, or that his chances of being caught are least in the largest cities with the highest crime rates. Roughly, a robber had one chance in two of being caught in 1955, but only one chance in three in 1975. This, however, is a higher risk of apprehension than what he would face in a large American city—there, he would have only one chance in four of being caught.

One reason for the greater risk facing the English robber may be found in the nature of his offense. Robbery is still a relatively infrequent crime, and so far as one can tell, it is disproportionately practiced by professional or semiprofessional criminals. One might think that the professional could, by his skill, more easily evade detection than the amateur, but in fact whatever advantage the professional acquires by virtue of craftiness is offset by his tendency to repeat the crime (thereby increasing his risk of apprehension in any given year) and to work with confederates (thus putting him at the mercy of potential informants).

A dramatic example occurred recently of the way in which the police can capitalize on these aspects of professional crime. In 1972, there were 72 bank robberies in London (there were 183 in New York that year). By 1974, Scotland Yard had cut that number to 17—a drop of better than 75 per cent.[19] As it turned out, most of the bank robberies were committed by one or two major gangs, one member of which turned Queen's evidence in return for a promise of leniency in his own case. He implicated his associates, who were arrested and given long prison terms. In the United States, by contrast, a large number of banks are robbed by lone wolves, acting almost on impulse, who may evade capture for long periods. And ordinary street muggings, in London as well as in New York, are the impulsive acts of young offenders and thus difficult to check by police strategies alone.

The ability of the English police to reduce crime may also be assisted by the kinds of legal powers they possess, powers in some important respects more ample than those of the American police; for example, a constable may stop and search any person he reasonably suspects of carrying arms, dangerous drugs, or stolen goods. An American officer in most jurisdictions would be limited to frisking suspicious persons for weapons ("patting them down"); to search beyond this, and to seize drugs or stolen goods, could only be done legally if the search were pursuant to a warrant or incident to a lawful arrest (which in turn requires that the crime be committed in the officer's presence or that the officer have probable cause—and not mere suspicion—that a felony had been committed by the person about to be arrested).

Furthermore, an English officer may enter a building without a warrant and search the premises in which he reasonably suspects that a person who has committed a crime is hiding. An American officer would be well advised to obtain a warrant before entering a building, even if he has probable cause to believe that there is a suspect inside.

Finally, in England an arrested person has the right to speak to an attorney (a "solicitor"), "provided that no hindrance is reasonably likely to be caused to the processes of investigation, or the administration of justice by his doing so."[20] In other words, the police may exclude a solicitor from the questioning of an arrested person. In America, such an exclusion is permissible only if agreed to by the accused.

Perhaps of greatest importance to the operation of the English police system is that evidence gathered in violation of the rules will not automatically be excluded from the trial—in theory, no one goes free merely because the constable has blundered.[21] The constable, on the other hand, is liable for serious civil, administrative, and criminal penalties if he acts improperly. Nor is this merely a theoretical possibility. In 1974, 84 London officers were prosecuted and 51 were found guilty of various offenses; in another 116 cases, disciplinary action was taken. Over ninety officers resigned from the force before the completion of a criminal or disciplinary inquiry.[22]

The American courts have used a different system to control the police: Exclude from a trial improperly gathered evidence in order, so the theory goes, to reduce the incentive for using improper means. No one can measure the extent to which the exclusionary rule as enforced in the United States results in lower rates of arrest and conviction and thus higher rates of crime. In routine cases—the burglar caught in the act, the robber identified by an eyewitness, the assaulter accused by his victim—the rule probably makes little difference. In more complex cases, where searches and interrogations are required, it may make some difference. In cases involving no complaining witness, such as drug violations, the rule may be of decisive importance.

Crime has not been the only problem to face the British police. Since 1972, there have been over 1,300 public demonstrations in greater London, 54 of which involved disorder resulting in the arrest of over 600 persons. Nearly 300 police officers were injured, as were a large but unknown number of participants and spectators. One demonstration, at Red Lion Square in June 1974, was especially difficult and ugly. A right-wing group, the National Front, sent about 900 persons on a march; about 1,000 left-wing opponents staged a countermarch; nearly 1,000 police officers were on hand; 51 persons were arrested, 54 were injured, and there was 1 fatality.[23]

Here, as with ordinary crime, the British police enjoy somewhat greater powers than their American counterparts. A demonstrator in London may be arrested for using threatening, abusive, or insulting words, or for carrying a sign displaying such words, or for using indecent language. American officers could not ordinarily make lawful arrests on such charges. They may, of course, arrest people for such behavior, but the charge must be for a real or claimed breach of a valid statute, such as resisting arrest or disorderly conduct.

The London police are upset by the violence that increasingly confronts them and with the behavior of the courts in punishing it. About 3,000 London bobbies were assaulted in 1974, an increase of 12 per cent over 1973. Sir Robert Mark, commissioner of the Metropolitan Police (Scotland Yard), is openly critical of the penalties given—or not given—to unlawful and violent demonstrators. Of the 758 charges brought against demonstrators during the past three years, 575 resulted in convictions, but only 18 in prison sentences, and of these, 12 were for only one month. Only 10 of the 105 convictions for assaulting a police officer produced imprisonment.[24] "The ability to maintain a satisfactory standard of public order in its widest sense is impaired . . . by pusillanimous laws and pusillanimous courts," Mark declared in August 1975.[25]

Despite the rise in violent crime, the advent of terrorism in London, the continued wave of disorderly demonstrations, the frequent injury to police officers, and the in-

creased use of firearms by criminals, there appears to be no
sentiment for arming the police. "Nothing could be sillier
or more irresponsible," Mark recently said to the officers at
the Bramshill Police College, "than to suggest in public
that in the forseeable future the police are likely to be
armed as a routine measure. There has never been less likelihood or justification for such a proposal . . . this is a proposal with which the overwhelming majority of policemen
would probably refuse to comply."[26]

Just as the London police are increasingly finding themselves, contrary to custom and legend, in an adversary role
with the citizenry, so also are they discovering that, contrary to custom and legend, not all their ranks are models
of integrity and rectitude. In February 1972, just two
months before Mark became the new commissioner, two
Scotland Yard detectives were sentenced at the Old Bailey
criminal courts to long prison terms for corruption. On taking office, Mark was appalled by what he saw and even
more by what he suspected. "I don't know what they [the
detectives] do to the enemy," he said, "but by God they
frighten me."[27] Mark, like most reform-minded police com-
missioners anywhere, soon discovered that the detective
service is a separate, virtually autonomous unit of the force
with its own leaders and rules. Peter Brodie, for six years
head of the Criminal Investigation Department (CID), was
widely thought to have the inside track for the post of commissioner. When Mark, a man who had never served in the
ranks of the Metropolitan Police (he had been chief constable in Leicester), was appointed instead, Brodie resigned. Mark promptly drew the battle lines with the CID,
threatening to put its entire membership back in uniform,
giving command over detectives to uniformed officers at
local police stations, creating a new unit (A10) to investigate complaints against officers, and requiring that meetings between detectives and informers be reported to superior officers.

The head of the Flying Squad was suspended from duty on charges of having gone on a Cyprus holiday with James Humphreys, the alleged "Emperor of Pornography" in London; the officer then resigned from the force. Humphreys himself boasted that he had 40 Scotland Yard men in his pocket. Of the 40, 22 have resigned, 12 are under investigation, and 6 were cleared. In all, Mark and the A10 unit investigated over a thousand cases against officers, with more to come. As of June 1975, 22 officers had been convicted on bribery or corruption charges, 20 awaited trial, and 12 had been acquitted, though 9 of the 12 plus another 45 officers not formally charged had been suspended from duty or otherwise disciplined. Over 300 officers had resigned in the face of investigations.[28]

None of this should have been surprising. It would be astonishing were it otherwise. Detectives in every force depend on informers to solve crimes. To acquire informers requires cultivating criminals. To make an arrest often requires inducing an informer to co-operate, and it is inevitable that in some cases improper means—planting evidence, using force—should be used to secure that co-operation. The London police, like their colleagues in New York, must enforce laws dealing with a number of so-called victimless crimes. The supposedly enlightened British policy of tolerating prostitution but banning solicitation, of allowing gambling but only on licensed premises, and of permitting government clinics to prescribe heroin for addicts has by no means eliminated the opportunities for police corruption or abuse of power in dealing with prostitutes, gamblers, pornographers, or drug users. Indeed, to a casual visitor, the abundance of obscene publications suggests that their illegality is not a matter of utmost concern to the police, just as the bewildering and often meaningless laws governing the licensing of and membership in gambling and night clubs seem almost an invitation for abuse and manipulation.

Mark is convinced that the system of justice is unduly biased in favor of the guilty. He would like to see a higher proportion of those who face trial be convicted, arguing that 40 per cent of those who plead innocent are acquitted, a proportion he believes unrealistically high. In all of this, he has encountered fierce opposition. His critics, among them Lord Wigoder, an officer of the Criminal Bar Association, and Michael Zander, an author and member of the London School of Economics, argue that juries are not often wrong, much less, as Mark put it, "occasionally stupid, prejudicial, and barely literate."

The vigorous argument between Mark and Zander over the acquittal rate of juries has stimulated some interesting research on jury behavior. In my view the data thus far do not show that the English juries are unreasonably inclined to acquit serious offenders. Of greater interest to an American, however, is the remarkable importance the jury retains in the British criminal justice system. In 1973, according to Zander, 40 per cent of the persons charged in English Crown Court pleaded not guilty, and thus were tried before a jury. In the same year, fewer than 9 per cent of the persons proceeded against on felony charges in California Superior Court saw a jury—the rest were handled by the judge acting alone, usually on the basis of a guilty plea. Plea bargaining in America has drastically reduced the frequency of trials, with or without a jury.

SENTENCING AND CORRECTIONS

The English response to rising crime rates during the 1960s appears, in the aggregate, to have been quite different from that in the United States. In America, the combined state and federal prison population declined from about 213,000 persons in 1960 to about 196,000 in 1970—a drop of approximately 9 per cent.[30] In England

and Wales, however, the average daily population of prisons increased from 20,857 in 1961 to 25,634 in 1970, a rise of about 23 per cent.[31]

These changes in the size of the prison population might lead one to suppose that British judges, unlike their American counterparts, responded to rising crime rates by getting tougher. That would be quite misleading. The English prison population may have gone up because judges became more severe, because there were more criminals being brought before judges who had a constant or even declining propensity to imprison, or because the kinds of crime being committed were becoming more serious.

Two things can be said: First, the chances of going to prison for having committed a serious crime are much greater in England than in America (which may help to explain why English crime rates are lower than American ones). Second, the chances of going to prison for having committed a serious offense are declining in England (which may help to explain why English crime rates are rising).

Take robbery, a major crime with a more or less common definition in the two countries. Because there are no national data in the United States on court dispositions, I shall compare England's experience with that of California, a state with relatively good statistics. In England in 1971, 26 per cent of the reported robberies resulted in some form of confinement—prison, detention center, or Borstal (reformatory).[32] In California in 1970, only 4 per cent of the robberies resulted in persons being put in custody in a jail, prison, or juvenile camp.[33] Stated another way, England, which had only one sixth the number of reported robberies, actually sent more persons to prison or its equivalent than was the case in California.

This does not mean that English judges are six times as severe as California ones. There are, roughly speaking, two kinds of courts: the major trial courts (in California, Superior Court; in England, Crown Court) and the lesser courts, which dispose of cases summarily or handle juveniles (in California, Municipal or Juvenile Court; in England, Magistrates' Court). If one looks only at the Superior or the Crown Court, it is not clear that English and American judges are very different. For example, among robbers appearing before Superior or Crown Court judges, about the same proportion (well over 80 per cent) were convicted, and of these about the same proportion (perhaps three fourths) received some form of custodial sentence. (Unfortunately, we cannot compare the length of the sentences, since that is not reported in California, though it is in England.)

The differing degrees of risk for robbers in the two countries are to be explained less by the behavior of trial court judges than by what happens to those robbers who never appear in the major trial courts at all—because they are not caught by the police, or are released by the prosecutor without charges, or are handled by the lesser courts, or are treated as juveniles. In England a robbery is more likely to be solved by an arrest than in California, a person arrested is more likely to be prosecuted, and a person prosecuted in a local court or as a juvenile is more likely to be confined. Any exact comparison of British and American dispositions is impossible, of course, since the American data are nonexistent. But it would appear that a major reason why the risk of crime is higher in England is that young offenders, who account for a large fraction of all crime, are treated more severely than in the United States.

Though the risks facing a criminal in England are high, they have been getting smaller. In 1966, 2,146 persons were brought into court charged with robbery. The great majority—85 per cent—were handled in Crown Court (then called Court of Assizes and Quarter Sessions). Of these, over 90 per cent were convicted; of those convicted, 60 per cent were sent to prison and another 25 per cent placed in Borstals or detention centers. Only 11 per cent were given some nonc̄ustodial sentence. For those going to prison, the typical sentence was two to three years. Nearly a third were sentenced for over three years. So far, the image of English justice seems confirmed: certain penalties, firmly applied.

The handful of robbers dealt with in Magistrates' Court were treated quite differently. Though nearly 90 per cent were found guilty, only 38 per cent of these were given some custodial sentence (a detention center or school for a few months), and none was sent to prison. No doubt the youth of these offenders played an important part in their more lenient treatment.

By 1974, the pattern had changed substantially. In that year 3,651 persons were brought into court charged with robbery. But owing in part to the fact that young persons now made up a much larger proportion of those committing robberies, a greater fraction—nearly a third—of these cases were handled in Magistrates' Court. Of those tried in Crown Court, about the same proportion as in 1966 were convicted, but a somewhat lower percentage of these were sent to prison—51 per cent in 1974, compared with 60 per cent in 1966. The prison terms were comparable in the two years. But in Magistrates' Court, the proportion found guilty was lower (79 per cent in 1974, compared with 89 per cent in 1966), and of those convicted, a smaller proportion were given custodial sentences (20 per cent in 1966 compared with 38 per cent in 1966). And whereas this more lenient treatment affected only about 300 accused robbers in 1966, it now affected over 1,000 in 1974.

In short, the probability that an accused robber would be given a custodial sentence in England and Wales fell from 62 chances out of 100 in 1966 to 47 chances out of 100 in

1974. The proportion of reported robberies, rather than of prosecuted robbers, that results in a custodial sentence is, of course, even smaller, and has also been declining—from 30 chances in 100 in 1966 to 20 chances in 100 in 1974.

It is unlikely that these changes in sentencing patterns are the result of any centrally made decision. The English judiciary, like the American, is constitutionally independent of executive authority and, again like the American, is not organized or staffed to devise and implement uniform sentencing policies. Since the early 1960s, there have been annual conferences of English judges at which sentencing was discussed and, since 1966, a newly appointed magistrate must take a training course that includes sentencing exercises. The Home Office also has published a handbook on sentencing. For all that, however, there remain substantial disparities in sentencing, and for essentially the same reason that they exist in the United States—courses, conferences, and handbooks are all very well, but when public officials are given substantial discretionary power, they will not surrender it, they will use it. Sentencing conferences have not been effective in this country, and there is little reason to suppose they are more effective abroad.

This would certainly explain why there appears to be as much disparity among the sentences of various judges in England as there is in other countries. One study, for example, showed that the proportion of young persons given probation was 12 per cent in one town and 79 per cent in a neighboring one.[34] Another study found equally wide disparities among Magistrates' Courts dealing with juveniles in London; still another found wide differences in the proportion of adults sent to prison by Magistrates' Courts throughout England and Wales.[35]

Nonetheless, the broad changes in English sentencing patterns, however unevenly they are proceeding, seem consistent with, if not dictated by, the policies of English governments extending back well into the last century. The rehabilitative ideal has been the object of the same veneration in England as in America. Originally that ideal was to be sought within the penitentiary. The Gladstone Report of 1895 urged that prisons be designed to develop the "moral instincts" of their inmates and thus to "turn them out better men and women, physically and mentally, than when they came in." But soon rehabilitation was thought to require nonprison alternatives. Borstals for "youth training" were created. But most important, the "major objective of English penal policy" came to be, as Richard F. Sparks has written, "to keep as many offenders as possible out of prison."[36]

A major step in the direction of increased reliance on noncustodial policies was the Criminal Justice Act of 1967, authorizing a court to suspend a sentence of imprisonment that does not exceed two years and, even more importantly, *requiring* that sentences not in excess of six months be suspended unless the offense was a violent one or certain other conditions were met. A Parole Board was also created, authorized to release from prison persons who had served one third of their sentences (or twelve months, whichever was greater). In 1972, another Criminal Justice Act was passed that modified the 1967 law—suspended sentences were no longer mandatory, but still strongly urged. It also instructed judges not to sentence anyone to prison who had not already been there unless they were satisfied that no other method of dealing with him was "appropriate."

Noncustodial treatment programs became very popular among British penal reformers of all political persuasions. Sir Arthur Peterson, then the permanent secretary (that is, senior civil servant) at the Home Office, was reported in 1973 as expressing doubts about the value of prison even for protecting society from offenders, and as hoping that falling crime rates (they did decline, briefly, in 1973 before rising sharply again) would reduce opposition to the further development of noncustodial programs.[37] The California Treatment Program, which had been praised (prematurely, as it turns out) by President Johnson's Crime Commission, was also widely hailed in England. In 1970, William F. Deedes, then a Conservative Member of Parliament and now the editor of the *Daily Telegraph,* endorsed the CTP approach—intensive probation and treatment programs for offenders returned to the community rather than sent to prison—unaware that as he spoke a reanalysis of the CTP data in the United States showed that claims for its crime-reduction potential had been vastly exaggerated.[38]

A policy of decarceration was supported by Robert Carr, Conservative Home Secretary, and continued by Roy Jenkins, his Labour successor. In late 1975, the Home Office Planning Unit described to an interviewer its major task as being to find a way of reducing the size of the prison population, partly to save money and end overcrowding but also, it frankly admitted, because of the ideological view that prison is an inappropriate way of dealing with offenders.

Despite the hope that prison populations could be reduced, they have in fact grown. This is not the result of the sentencing practices of judges but of the rise in the number of crimes being committed; on this, the careful studies of Richard F. Sparks are quite conclusive.[39] Indeed, if the harsher prewar sentencing practices were still in effect, the prison population would be vastly larger than it is today. In 1968, for example, about three fifths of all those in prison were discharged after only four months.[40] Furthermore, as in the United States, those sent to prison tend to have many previous convictions, though often not many previous prison sentences. Of the more than 2,000 adult men sent to prison in 1967 for having committed a violent crime (other than murder), over 87 per cent had one prior conviction and over 55 per cent had five or more prior convictions. Despite these long records, over a third had never been in prison before and over half had only been in once.[41]

England would seem ripe for the kind of debate that has recently developed in the United States over the crime-reduction potential of prisons, either by virtue of their deterrent effect on would-be offenders or their incapacitative effect on actual ones. As yet no informed debate on this issue has emerged, in part because official circles in England are less willing than those in the United States to concede the inefficacy of rehabilitation. In America, persons of both parties and at all levels of government are aware of and have taken fully into account the findings of Robert Martinson and others that rehabilitation programs, non-custodial as well as custodial, have been ineffective.[42] No such recognition has yet been expressed by comparable British officials, even though British scholars—notably Roger Hood, Leslie Wilkins, and Sir Rupert Cross—have come to almost precisely the same conclusions as their American counterparts.

Where British scholarship has lagged has not been in studies of recidivism but in those on deterrence. Statistical analyses in the United States have consistently though not conclusively supported the view that the higher the probability of arrest and imprisonment in a given jurisdiction, the lower the crime rate, other things (such as the characteristics of the population) being equal. I am aware of only one British study of this sort—a 1973 paper by R. A. Carr-Hill and N. H. Stern. Applying the customary econometric techniques to data for the police districts of England and Wales, they found that, other things being equal, the greater the probability of arrest, the lower the rate of indictable offenses. There was also a significant, though weaker, relationship between imprisonment and crime—the higher the proportion of convicted persons receiving custodial sentences, the lower the offense rate. These results are similar to those obtained with American data, yet there has been little effort in England either to test further the approach or to weigh seriously its policy implications. The Home Office, which boasts a Research Unit and a Statistical Unit as well as a Planning Unit, does not seem inclined to pursue this line of inquiry.

Instead of attempting, soberly and carefully, to analyze the criminal justice system to discover and measure such effects as it might have on crime rates under alternative sentencing policies, the English seem instead on the verge of a major ideological brawl between "liberal" and "conservative" opinion. The chairman of the Howard League, Louis Blom-Cooper, and others are vigorously advocating abolition of prison for all but the most dangerous criminal offenders; they are pressing instead for greater reliance on "a continuing programme of adjustment" based on "the control and supervision of offenders within the community" —with terms to be set not by judges, but by administrative authorities who would decide which, if any, of the offenders "needed" confinement. The treatment perspective, the indeterminate sentence, and the use of (never clearly specified) "community" resources is a view very much alive and well in England; the report of the Advisory Council on the Penal System regarding young offenders goes far in this direction, though not quite as far as Mr. Blom-Cooper, a member of the Council who dissented from the report, would like.[43]

At the opposite end of the spectrum is Sergeant Leslie Male, chairman of the Police Federation, who is calling, on behalf of his organization, for more police, more prisons, and more jail sentences instead of fines, in order to counter the "frightening" increase in crime.[44]

At issue are not simply the questions of public safety vs.

prisoner amenity and deterrence vs. rehabilitation, but questions of justice. Roger Hood, at Oxford, for example, favors shorter prison sentences, but he argues that terms should be set by judges on the basis of determinate sentences and legal criteria, not by administrators on the basis of indeterminate sentences and therapeutic objectives.[45] It is a view that has come to be widely held in the United States, but official circles in England tend to dismiss it by referring to Hood, wearily, as "that due process fellow."

CRIME AND BRITISH POLITICS

Thus far the primacy of economic issues and (by American standards) the infrequency of serious violent crime have permitted the debate over the criminal justice system in England to proceed sedately, in measured tones, among a small group of attentive observers. The complaints of Sir Robert Mark and the far tougher statements of the Police Federation may be harbingers of what is to come, if crime continues to rise at its present rate and if each governmental commission examining the matter continues to respond by devising new ways of putting offenders back on the street as quickly as possible.

British politics handles crime differently from American politics, and not simply because the British have less violent crime. Party control of nominations for seats in the House of Commons and the absence of much in the way of an independent local government reduce significantly the opportunity or incentive for a person to launch or expand a political career by developing a following around a certain issue. There are a number of American politicians who have used "crime in the streets" as an issue, often with success; such behavior is far less likely in England. Political advancement comes more from party conformity than from popular appeals. On the other hand, American elected officials have had great difficulty in changing the American criminal justice system—the very decentralization, party weakness, and governmental fragmentation that make issue appeals so rewarding make legislative or administrative action on the basis of those appeals so difficult. The major federal piece of legislation—the Safe Streets Act of 1968—changed little in the criminal-justice system except the amount of federal money spent on it. There have been a number of changes at the state level, but of a piecemeal and often inconsistent nature.

British public officials, though not attracted by the political appeal of crime, can, as members of the majority party, participate in making substantial changes when they are so inclined. The entire criminal courts system was reorganized by the Courts Act of 1971, sentencing rules were altered substantially by the Criminal Justice Act of 1967 and again by the Criminal Justice Act of 1972, and capital punishment was abolished by the Murder Act of 1965. It would be unthinkable—and perhaps unconstitutional—for such sweeping national changes to be voted by the U. S. Congress. Yet in the arena where changes might occur—the states—the appropriate agencies are poorly staffed, and even knowledge of current policy is lacking, to say nothing of good ideas about future practice.

However greater the British political capacity to act, that capacity has not yet extended to devoting significantly greater resources to criminal justice—the police are understaffed and the number and variety of correctional institutions and programs are inadequate. Even the British tradition of a speedy trial has suffered under the crush of business in the major Crown Courts. In 1973, a person being proceeded against in the Old Bailey—the Central Criminal Court in London—had to wait more than six months for a trial if he were out on bail and nearly four months if he were in custody.[46] Most importantly, the inclination to test carefully the consequences for crime of alternative sentencing policies does not yet seem great.

If English virtue is collapsing, at least as measured by the crime rate, it is not doing so under the weight of political turmoil and economic crisis. Crime began going up in the 1950s, long before Britain's problems became as grave as they are today. But the present problems are straining the country's ability to respond to crime and perhaps impeding its ability to think about them.

The Failure of the Conservative Party, 1945–75

Patrick Cosgrave

The British Conservative Party is historically both unique
and astonishing. It has a defined identity reaching back into
the seventeenth century, and its origins can be traced back
to even earlier dates. Moreover, survival has not been its
only triumph: It has either governed, or shared in the government of, Britain for long stretches of its history, and has
always been supremely adaptable to the twists and turns of
history. It has changed its nature and policies many times:
From being isolationist in the seventeenth century, it became imperial in the nineteenth century. It has been a party
of the aristocracy, of the squirearchy, and of business. And
in the twentieth, the century of the common man, it has
until recently dominated the government of the country. So
accustomed are Tories to being in office that unreasoning
fits of hysterics commonly seize them when they lose it. Despair was the note of Conservative politics when the election of 1964 ended thirteen years of their rule. Much more
genuinely serious, however, has been the Conservative experience since 1970: Upon its unexpected return to power
in June of that year, imbued with a newly doctrinal reforming instinct, the party and its leader, Mr. Edward Heath,
proceeded to waste the substance of its triumph, and was
twice defeated in 1974. To any casual observer the party
seemed, even under a new leader, deeply divided on policy

matters, to which were added sharp rifts among some of its leading personalities.

Of course, some would argue that none of this needs to be taken too seriously, for the Conservative Party has frequently seemed in deep trouble before, and events have always conspired to rescue it. In the eighteenth and nineteenth centuries alike it had to endure long years of opposition, and the split between Peel and Disraeli, which led to one of those exiles, was far deeper, and of far greater consequence, than any division that existed between Mrs. Thatcher and Mr. Heath. Even in the present century, the Liberal triumph in the general election of 1906—in which the Conservative leader and then Prime Minister, Arthur Balfour, lost his seat—seemed to ensure a lengthy period of aridity for the Conservatives, especially when the Liberals held onto power in the elections of 1911. But the war came, the Tories joined a coalition and, within five years of the armistice, the Liberal Party was shattered beyond repair and the Conservatives were back in power. In the great crisis that began in 1929 the Conservatives were again in opposition, but 1931 saw their rescue, again through the agency of coalition; and they dominated government in the thirties. Even the shattering defeat of 1945, when many seasoned observers saw the triumph of Labour as the dawn of a new progressive era, was followed only six years later by a thirteen-year span of Tory power.

With this history it was hardly surprising that many optimistic Conservatives saw no particular difficulty in their 1974 circumstances, and trusted to an almost mystic belief in the durability of their party and the certainty of its return to power. It was hardly surprising, either, that so many Conservatives—principally those still attached to Mr. Heath—saw their salvation in coalition, for that was the method of rescue twice already in this century; thus, having fought the election of February 1974 on a policy of confrontation, and having lost it, the Tories fought that of October on a policy of conciliation. "After the election," Mr. Heath's manifesto read, "we will consult and confer with the leaders of other parties and with the leaders of the great interests in the nation, in order to secure for the Government's policies the consent and support of all men and women of goodwill. We will invite people from outside the ranks of our party to join with us in overcoming Britain's difficulties."

Alas for Mr. Heath, the country did not heed his appeal, and he was replaced as leader by Mrs. Margaret Thatcher, who had all along resolutely opposed the idea of coalition. The importance of Mrs. Thatcher's leadership is not simply that it is an innovation, nor that she is temperamentally and intellectually opposed to consensus and conciliation in political method; it is also that a number of her personal supporters have been highly critical, not merely of the record of the Heath years, but of most of the Conservative record since the war.

There was always a strong subterranean critique of the Conservative leadership, even in the halcyon days of Mr. Harold Macmillan, but much of it was made up of the views of what might be called the Old Right—those whose emotions and thinking were bound up with the idea of Britain as an imperial power and who were convinced that the Macmillan retreat from colonial positions was unnecessary, ill-timed, and disastrous. There was also what might be called the New Right, which wanted to reduce public spending and taxation, and to encourage capitalism, free enterprise, and personal freedom. Under Mr. Macmillan three ministers, Mr. Peter Thorneycroft, Mr. Enoch Powell, and Mr. Nigel Birch, resigned from the Treasury because they were opposed to the level of public spending. But it was not until the middle sixties, when they were encouraged by Mr. Heath, that their ideas gained any promi-

nence in the party generally, and from 1968 onward Mr.
Powell blazed a trail outside the Tory establishment for
what was accurately understood to be an ideological, doctrinal conservatism, much more akin to the American than
to the traditional British. Mr. Powell remains out of favor,
but he undoubtedly prepared the way for Mrs. Thatcher
and her close ally, Sir Keith Joseph, to assert more moderate versions of his own doctrine of economic liberalism,
and repudiate the heritage of postwar conservatism. The
disasters that befell Mr. Heath's government—as inflation
became rampant, as public spending rose, and as controls
over incomes were introduced in direct defiance of an electoral pledge—gained the New Right great influence within
the party.

Thus is the stage set for battle, not only in Britain as a
whole, but also within the Conservative Party itself. Essentially it is now a dispute between those who believe that the
party should not be ideological, should accept most of the
changes introduced by the Labour Party when it is in
power, and should strive to administer society humanely
when it gains office, and those on the other hand who believe that, given the present growth of state socialism and
its resulting woes, radical policies are needed if the tide is
to be reversed. The real leader of the first group is Mr.
Heath, but its senior thinker is Mr. Ian Gilmour, who actually sits in Mrs. Thatcher's shadow Cabinet. The members
of the second group, with which Mrs. Thatcher is more or
less identified, see little point in office without power to in-
augurate fundamental changes, and they believe that only
such Conservative changes will save Britain; their ideology
thus hopes to awaken the old identification of the Conservative Party with patriotism. The intellectual leader of this
group is Sir Keith Joseph, but Mr. Powell is in the wings.
Historically, the most interesting aspect of the emergence
of the New Right is that it tends to select for praise as the

only genuinely successful Tory government since the war
an administration long regarded as part of a moribund
twilight—the last Churchill government (1951–55), presided over by a failing but still cunning great leader, and
the government that, of all since the war, has appropriated
the smallest percentage of personal income in taxation. Interestingly, the first Chancellor of the Exchequer in that
government, R. A.—now Lord—Butler, who pursued a
policy of economic liberalism, was also the man who
presided over the coming to terms of the Conservative
Party with the achievements of modern socialism immediately after the war; and it is to that period of Conservative
reaction to overwhelming defeat that we must now turn.

When Clement Attlee's Labour government was elected
in 1945, its two great objectives were, first, to establish the
control of the state over the "commanding heights" of the
economy and, second, to take large-scale and institu-
tionalized steps—like the establishment of the National
Health Service, giving free health care to all the people—
for improving the welfare of the citizenry. Three factors
strongly affected the Conservatives' response. The first was
a long tradition of Conservative support for the welfare
state. In the nineteenth century it was almost invariably the
Conservative Party that advocated state intervention for
improving the condition of the people. The most powerful
advocate of social reform was the great Tory radical, Lord
Shaftesbury, who, though we would nowadays call him an
extreme rightist on everything else, sponsored innumerable
major schemes of social improvement. Disraeli stated the
achievement of such schemes as his major objective in domestic politics. The Liberals, who believed in a totally lais-
sez-faire policy, invariably opposed the Tories; and it was
not until the rise of Lloyd George in the early twentieth
century that the Liberal Party became involved in welfare

politics. In the 1920s and 1930s, the Conservative Party was less interventionist. Even so, the Conservative Neville Chamberlain was perhaps the best Health Minister of the whole pre-1945 period, and a dissident Conservative group, led by Harold Macmillan and inspired by his book *The Middle Way*, favored much more developed intervention than the Conservative leadership; in particular Macmillan and his followers were deeply grieved by the phenomenon of unemployment, about which Conservative governments did very little. Conservatives helped to draft many of the 1945 Labour Government's welfare measures by participating in the all-party committees working on welfare questions during the war; this applies in particular to the National Health Service and to the development of state-dominated education, enshrined in R. A. Butler's Education Act of 1944, the Act under which governments of both parties have ever since worked. It was therefore very difficult for the Conservative Party to offer any critique in principle of the welfare measures the Attlee government was taking in 1945 and afterward; criticisms were merely of timing, tactics, and expense.

Second, it seemed perfectly clear in 1945 that the country wanted a much more radical shift in economic and social policy than it was believed the Conservative Party was willing to provide. A great part of this instinct was undoubtedly based on the horrible memories of the thirties and on the conviction that a New Jerusalem should be built after the sufferings of the war. Even so, the desire for change should not be exaggerated, for the British electoral system magnifies in terms of parliamentary seats a numerical advantage in numbers of votes. It sounded terrifying to the Conservatives that, in 1945, Labour had gained 393 seats to their own 213, especially when one remembered that the National Government (of Tories and Labour but with the main body of the Labour Party opposed) had, in 1931, enjoyed an over-all majority of 496 seats, and in 1935 of 248. But Labour had in 1945 nonetheless gained only a 10 per cent lead in the polls, and that meant only about 1.7 million votes more than the Conservatives in an electorate of nearly 33 million, more than 72 per cent of whom voted. The swing required in 1950 to reduce the huge Labour majority to a mere 17 was only 3.13 per cent. It can thus be argued that the Conservative position in 1945 was much better than it appeared. Nonetheless, the party was frightened and, given the rise to influence of both Macmillan and Butler, and the considerable sympathy of Churchill himself for welfare policies—he and Lloyd George had laid the foundations of the modern welfare state in the 1906 Liberal government —the hunt was on, after 1945, for aspects of the Labour program that the Conservatives could accept, rather than for an effective critique of it. I am not here arguing that the Conservatives could safely have opposed, as arrant social-ism, the introduction of the welfare state, for the national desire for social improvement was undoubtedly powerful. But there were different ways of doing things: The wartime Health Service scheme was, for example, very different from that eventually adopted by Aneurin Bevan, and Iain Macleod made his political reputation—and gained the Ministry of Health for himself—by saying so with great effect in the 1951 Parliament. The wartime plan was prob-ably superior, but the Conservatives made no attempt radi-cally to alter the Bevan structure after their return to power in 1951. They were not, on their historical record, opposed in principle to its provisions; and their attitude after 1945 established a pattern of consensus (only slightly fractured after the election of Mr. Heath in 1970) whereby the Con-servative Party sought to alter as little as possible the gov-ernment structure that they inherited in 1951, and in some respects they even sought to expand it.

Third, this consensus was to hold even in economic matters: Between 1945 and 1950 the Conservative Party resolved to accept at least in part the principles of intervention in the economy established by Attlee. This was not a mindless acceptance. The Tories would leave in state hands such industries as mining and the railways, where it could be argued that private enterprise was incapable of providing services on the scale required, but they would denationalize such industries as steel where, they believed, private enterprise could cope sufficiently well. Thus was born the concept of a mixed economy, the broad character of which was accepted by both major parties. It was not until after 1970 that Labour abandoned the concept of the mixed economy; today, the followers of Mr. Anthony Wedgwood-Benn believe as a matter of socialist principle that successful, as well as unsuccessful, industry should be taken over by the state, though Mr. Wilson, Mr. Callaghan, and their allies prefer the state's taking shares in private industry to total nationalization. Even this marks a major change, however, from the policies advocated by the leading socialist theoretician of the 1950s and 1960s, Mr. Anthony Crosland, who specifically disavowed further nationalization. Especially after the failure of the Heath government, which had first broken with the consensus by announcing its determination not to sustain with public money ailing industrial enterprises, the Conservatives have found it difficult to erect an opposition of principle to the activities of a Labour government, and their failure to do so goes back to their decision, after 1945, to accept the main body of whatever economic legislation they found on their return to office. It did not follow that the Conservatives, after the war, abandoned their belief in freedom, low taxation, and the encouragement of enterprise—their slogan in the early fifties was "Set the People Free," and the second Churchill government abolished a whole series of controls, including food rationing, that Labour had sustained—but they preferred to do this through budgetary action (and Lord Butler did it brilliantly) rather than through structural reform.

The balance of instinct within the Conservative Party in 1945—the degree to which it stood for freedom, the degree to which it was prepared to sanction intervention— therefore came from no ideological or philosophical formulation, but from historical experience. Its problem was how to come to terms both with its defeat and with the things the victors were now about to do. For many years after 1951, when the Tories returned to power—probably, indeed, until 1974—the work of Lord Butler at the Conservative Research Department from 1945—assisted by a team of brilliant young men who were later to rise to prominence as Conservative politicians, including Mr. Reginald Maudling, Mr. Enoch Powell, and the late Iain Macleod—was regarded as the foremost glory of modern conservatism. What Lord Butler and his young men attempted—and what issued in such documents as *The Social Charter* and *The Industrial Charter*—was to regain the intellectual initiative for the Conservative Party by sorting out what in their own tradition was still relevant and what in the Labour Party's achievement realism counseled them to accept. As Lord Blake wrote,

> The Conservative revival was helped by an intellectual movement in their favour. *Etatisme* which had been all the rage in the 1930s lost its charm in the highly regimented England of the war and post-war years. A very influential book at the time was Professor F. A. Hayek's *Road to Serfdom,* published in 1944. It was essentially anti-Socialist in its implications. The universities saw a notable revival of Conservative sympathies among the undergraduates and to some extent among the dons too. The Conservative Research Department

headed by R. A. Butler contained as members during the period . . . people of whom many things have been said, but not that they are stupid. The Labour Party had lost its near monopoly of intellect and ideas.[1]

So far I have concentrated on the Conservative reaction to the triumph of Labour in terms of its moral and intellectual reaction to Labour's program. There are two reasons for this. First, the nature and extent of the Labour victory, and the determination with which Attlee and his colleagues set about their task of fundamental reform established a totally new pattern of British political life, and the Conservatives had either to come to terms with it or try to overthrow it. Second, as the years have gone by since 1945, as the Empire has withered away and Britain's preoccupations have become more domestic, the confrontation of 1945–51 has deepened, especially as the country's economic prospects declined. The most vigorous Labour politicians have become increasingly discontented with their inheritance from Attlee and have deliberately dedicated themselves to extending the role of the state in economic, welfare, and educational matters. The most vigorous Tories have gone in exactly the opposite direction, and the Conservative government of 1970 actually undertook, in the words of its leader, Mr. Edward Heath, "to change the course of history of this nation—nothing less." After the failure of the 1970 government, the Conservative Party was deeply divided between those who wanted to keep Mr. Heath's promise and those—including himself—who regarded the best option available to their party as the opportunity from time to time to administer a mainly socialist country as decently as possible by controlling incomes, subsidizing industry, and maintaining the welfare system. Of course, the failure of the Heath government had many causes, but the main result of that failure was to reproduce the debate of 1945–51 in a much more acute form, and in circumstances where many Conservatives were considering surrender to collectivism in a far more thoroughgoing fashion than was necessary or desirable in 1945. It is central to my thesis that the role of the Conservative intellectuals after 1945 has been exaggerated, for I do not believe they really thought through their response to Labour; rather, they erected a somewhat superficially glittering rhetoric, which convinced the electorate that the more popular elements of the Labour program were accepted, and thus allowed the Conservatives to play, without fear of being thought *revanchistes* in domestic politics, their stronger cards: the solidarity of the property-owning classes—including those with only very little property—the British dislike of regimentation, and patriotism, especially as symbolized by Churchill.

Lord Blake, in a passage full of wisdom, tries to analyze the development of British politics between 1945 and 1950, when the Conservatives almost returned to power. "The mass of the electorate," he writes,

was [in 1945] voting in defence of full employment, and against a reversion to the economic depression of the 1930s. To this sentiment was added the impetus of socialist utopianism inspired by the anti-capitalist writings of a whole intellectual generation. On neither level could the Conservatives bring anything like such strength to bear. In 1950 the defensive argument was still a very strong Labour asset. Indeed full employment was one of the party's main themes, and by far the smallest pro-Conservative swing occurred in the areas of high pre-war unemployment. But even on the defensive level the advantage did not lie wholly with Labour. Cripps's devaluation of the pound in 1949 operated in the opposite sense for obvious reasons. And on the positive level, that of party enthusiasm, the Conservatives undoubtedly had the edge over Labour. The various conflicting forces virtually cancelled each other out, in 1950.

Twenty months later with a swing of 1 per cent the Conservatives just managed to get in with a majority of 17 over all other parties but a minority of the total poll. No one can say why. Perhaps the fears of unemployment had become that much less. Perhaps the increased emphasis on Tory freedom, after another year and a half of restriction, made just the difference. "Set the people free" was an effective slogan. Combined with the *Industrial Charter* it gave the Conservatives a distinctive colour that was neither reactionary on the one hand nor a smudged copy of Labour's on the other. True, Labour itself had by now gone in for "a bonfire of controls." But it is seldom a good sign when a government starts adopting opposition policies, e.g., the abrupt conversion of the Conservatives in 1963–64 to planning and "modernisation."

The 1950s were a genuine watershed period in British history, for it was that decade—the decade of Suez—that saw the liquidation of the British Empire, a shattering retraction of the nation's intellectual and moral horizons, and the first move to submerge Britain's identity in a European federation. But that national self-disgust, the debilitating feeling of being a tiny island adrift like a cork on the ocean of world politics did not take hold until the middle sixties when the domestic economy had been for so long so mismanaged—partly because of the pursuit by both parties of collectivist policies, partly because the people had been trained to expect a continually expanding public provision of services which the country could not afford, partly because nobody appreciated the fact that a decline in Britain's international power would mean a decline in her wealth as well. Under Conservative leadership in the fifties, however, the British were comforted by illusions of continuing grandeur. First of all, the titanic international reputation of Churchill persuaded other countries that Britain's power was in most matters unaltered, until he retired in 1955. Second, Mr. Macmillan, who succeeded as Prime Minister in 1957, carried out the colonial withdrawal which seemed to him unavoidable, especially after the Suez debacle, with such skill and magic that people were almost persuaded that it made no difference, and that the Commonwealth was an adequate substitute for the Empire. Third, the dominating minds of the Labour Party were so closely and personally identified with the first generation of new leaders of the former colonial countries, most of whom had been trained in Britain and many of whom were members of the Labour Party, that the intimacy of relations convinced them that there was no need to bother about the possibility of African and Asian nations moving away from Britain. Fourth—and this was again due to the genius of Mr. Macmillan—the wound of Suez was quickly cauterized, when it might have opened a gaping hole in the nation's side; relations with the United States were repaired; and Britain set on a foreign policy course in agreement with the United States from which she has scarcely ever since diverged. Mr. Macmillan conjured up again the magic of the special relationship, not only with President Eisenhower but with President Kennedy, and managed to make it appear that Britain was still an almost equal partner with America.

Britain was not an equal partner, of course, and a failure to understand what was really happening to Britain internationally in the fifties was quite as much a cause of the trouble we find ourselves in today as any failure of the Conservative Party to mount an effective critique of socialism. True, coming near the Conservative defeat of 1964 there were indications that all was not well: there was a furious British reaction, for instance, to Dean Acheson's observation that Britain had lost an empire and not yet found

a role, a reaction out of all proportion to the real novelty of
the remark. But the more widespread note of political con-
versation in the fifties and early sixties was one of self-
congratulation, to the effect that Britain, unlike any other
possessor of a great empire of which history has record, had
been able to divest herself of masses of colonies which had,
since the late nineteenth century at least, been her moral
raison d'être, and all this without any notable effect on her
constitution or morale.

All this was, of course, to have a far more fundamental
effect on the Conservative than on the Labour Party, because the Tories were the party of Empire. And what in retrospect seems extraordinary about the activity of the Conservative Party in foreign affairs since the war is that they
clung to two propositions about international relations that
events had made untenable. The first of these was the conviction that the Commonwealth could replace the Empire;
the second that Britain should make sacrifices to maintain
the international parity of the pound sterling. So potent was
the second of these propositions that it dominated the domestic economic life and policy even of the 1966 government of Mr. Wilson; it seemed to both parties a sin that the
pound should be allowed to depreciate. As late as the 1970
general election the fact that the Attlee government had
been so wicked as to devalue was a potent weapon in the
hands of Conservative propagandists.

The first of the foreign policy propositions of postwar
Conservatism was given some degree of intellectual coher-
ence by Anthony Eden, Prime Minister from 1955 to
1957. While accepting that the Empire was lost, he
believed that Britain could continue to play a vital international role as supervisor of what he regarded as the triptych
of Europe, the United States, and the Commonwealth. This
illusion masquerading as a foreign policy Mr. Harold Macmillan, when he succeeded Eden, sedulously defended. It

was all a very long way from the *realpolitik* of the third Marquis of Salisbury, greatest of Tory leaders, longest serving Prime Minister of the nineteenth century, and the father of British isolation. Time conspired to erode the internationalist illusion: Far from replacing the Empire as a source of self-esteem the Commonwealth became a burden —especially when immigrants from Commonwealth states arrived in large numbers in Britain. Far from being a badge of international respectability, the maintenance of a steady parity for the pound imposed eventually unacceptable burdens on the domestic economy of Great Britain. The weight of that burden was realized when Labour was in power; but the devaluation of the pound which Mr. Harold Wilson eventually felt obliged to impose was fiercely resisted by Mr. Heath, though to him it was left to float the pound when he became, in his turn, Prime Minister. It is amazing and sad that the Conservatives, the party that could have most effectively combined realism and romanticism in international affairs, should, by some strange chemistry, have forgotten any serious appreciation of the national interest, and opted instead for dreams.

Thus in the international field, and in spite of the Suez trauma, the extent of Britain's decline was most skillfully concealed; while in domestic politics, and in spite of difficulties, a pattern of prosperity and success was established that led the Conservatives to an overwhelming victory in 1959. It was entirely appropriate that they should have been led at that election by Mr. Macmillan, for it was he who, responding to the gloom in which many Conservatives returned to office in 1951, observed,

> The truth is that the Socialists have fought the election (very astutely) not on Socialism but on fear. Fear of unemployment; fear of reduced wages; fear of reduced social benefits; fear of war. These four fears have been brilliantly, if un-

scrupulously exploited. If, before the next election, none of these fears have proved reasonable, we may be able to force the Opposition to fight on Socialism. Then we can win.

The Conservatives succeeded, and both in 1955 and 1959 were able to choose the ground of the battle. But their success was to be relative, to be a success in party political, rather than in national terms. I mentioned earlier that, between 1945 and 1951, the decision was taken within the leadership of the Conservative Party to sift through Labour's program to find what was acceptable there, and then to give to what was accepted a persuasive Tory intellectual gloss; there was to be no fundamental critique of the—as it now appears to us fairly moderate—socialism of Attlee. As Mr. Michael Harrington and Mr. T. F. Lindsay observe of the 1951 government,

> But the extent of the consensus should not be exaggerated. The Conservative Government laid emphasis on the reduction of taxation and on home ownership; ended many of the regulations imposed on private enterprise; and reduced public expenditure in proportion to the gross national product. These were moves away from egalitarian collectivism in the direction of economic individualism. But the movement was not sudden and dramatic, nor was it taken very far.[2]

That it was possible to gain any elbow room for tax reductions and the lifting of regulations at all was largely due to the exceptional skill of the Chancellor of the Exchequer, Mr. R. A. Butler. But even during his administration of the Exchequer (from 1951 to 1955), a pattern—which we now call stop-go—began to establish itself, with accelerating repetitions, in the workings of the British economy. Before the 1955 election Butler again reduced taxation. Not long after the election victory, however, he had to face the disparity between government income and government expenditure that has bedevilled all Chancellors since. The emergency budget in autumn 1955 increased taxation, reduced subsidies, and imposed spending restrictions. Again and again in the following years that pattern of relaxation and imposition repeated itself. By the time Mr. Macmillan became Prime Minister, many concerned economists and, more importantly, the three Treasury Ministers—Mr. Peter Thorneycroft, Mr. Nigel Birch, and Mr. Enoch Powell—were starting to give priority to their fears about inflation, and to express vigorously their conviction that its main cause was the imbalance between government expenditure and government income. In the preparation of the 1957 budget, however, which the Chancellor wished to make deflationary, an important and dangerous tension between the Prime Minister and his economic ministers emerged.

When he became Prime Minister, Mr. Macmillan had this to say of the course he intended to follow:

> I am slightly amused by the fact that during the early part of my life I was accused of leaning too much to the Left. I have seen recently accusations that I leaned too far to the Right.[3] I propose, as I have always, to follow the Middle Way.

To follow the middle way in 1957 meant essentially to defend that consensus the Conservatives had established between 1945 and 1951. Above all, it meant accepting certain propositions about social objectives, especially the goal of full employment. Between the wars the economist John Maynard Keynes had proposed the ideal of full employment as a wise and humane objective for all democratic governments, and he believed it could be financed in part at least by deficit financing. It is not necessary to go here into the complicated economic arguments for and against Keynes's thesis, but this much should be emphasized: By full employment he emphatically did not mean as low a number of people out of work for long periods as we mean by the same formulation today. If one remembers, further, that very many serious critics—including Sir Keith Joseph —take the view that traditional British governmental methods of measuring unemployment invariably exaggerate to a considerable extent the severity of the problem, one can begin to see how British governments since the war, and especially since 1957, have continually made their self-imposed task of maintaining full employment ever more difficult. In any event, unemployment, or the threat of it, always had a special emotional impact on Mr. Macmillan and, as 1957 wore on, he became stronger and stronger in his resistance to the desire for deflationary policies urged by his Treasury ministers, all three of whom resigned at the end of the year.

The tendency of today's Conservative intellectuals—and of Mrs. Thatcher—is to believe that the Treasury ministers were right, and the Prime Minister was wrong. Such has been one of the results of the growing influence of Professor Milton Friedman and the Chicago school on British politics in the intervening years, though to it has been added the influence of Mr. Powell both within and outside of the Conservative Party. But between 1957 and 1959, Mr. Macmillan—again showing imcomparable political skill—easily overcame the effect of the three ministerial resignations. There could be no question that, in spite of hiccups of varying seriousness in economic management, the consensus on which the Conservatives had entered between 1945 and 1951 had served Britain well, at least in material terms; and it was on the Conservative housing and social records in particular that the Party was able to win a tremendous victory—with a majority of 100 seats—in 1959.

In his 1959 government Mr. Macmillan faced three serious problems. First, his ministerial team was growing stale, and he was unwilling to change it; when he made drastic changes in 1962, it was already too late. Perhaps partly because of staleness, the government fell victim to a series of security and moral scandals. Difficulties and waning popularity were symbolized in the revival of the Liberal Party, whose victory at the Orpington by-election had, as Mr. Harrington and Mr. Lindsay observe, the important result of breaking the nerve of the Prime Minister.

Second, the ills that Mr. Thorneycroft and his friends had diagnosed did not go away; they multiplied. In an attempt to palliate them, Mr. Macmillan moved, not to the right, but to the left of the consensus. He adopted economic planning on a scale that no Conservative had ever dreamed of, and he imposed Britain's first, rudimentary, system of income control. This decision to use the power of the state to control the economy, and to intervene much more directly in the nation's affairs, was in no sense a panic move, however. It was the direct and deliberate selection of one element of the heritage the party had been steadily taking to itself since 1945. Those who denounced it then did so because, they declared, it was un-Conservative; but Mr. Macmillan was able to appeal to the pragmatic traditions of the historical Conservative Party, at a time, moreover, when it was widely believed that political ideology was dead, and that all future political debate in Britain would be within the pragmatic scale. Of course, the Conservative desire to intervene was very different from that of Labour —the British Labour Party believes in a collectivist ideology and in state action as a matter of principle. The elements in the party who would question its value—like Mr. Anthony Crosland, Labour's most influential theoretician in the fifties and sixties—do so purely on grounds of political unacceptability. Conservative interventionism has always been—though less so of late—reluctant to embrace social engineering; rather it has been confined to intervention in the economic process, without much regard to the social consequences of such intervention. But, to repeat the crucial point, Mr. Macmillan's decision to start a whole series of institutional controls over the economy, though not out of keeping with the recent past of his party, moved directly into territory in which the Labour Party was much happier than its rivals. In 1963 and 1964 it became increasingly clear that the electorate, if it wanted a collectivist party, was likely to prefer the one that had collectivism at the center of its creed. By the early 1960s all that stood between the Conservatives and their enemies was a widespread conviction that, while both parties agreed on the main lines of domestic policy and economic management, the Conservatives at least ran things better.

Here it would, perhaps, be useful to anticipate a little. In the right circumstances it can be a tremendous advantage for a party to hold office. Ministers, in an age of mass communication, have an enormous advantage over Opposition spokesmen in their capacity to make news and present themselves to the people. Tired though they may have been as long as they held office, the Conservatives found it easy to depict their rivals as wild-eyed revolutionaries. Once the spell is broken by an electoral defeat, however, it is the rival who assumes the magic of office. And the pattern of British politics since Labour gained the edge over the Conservatives in 1962—and with the exception of Mr. Heath's period of opposition from 1968 and his first year in office—has been for the magic to attach itself to Labour. There are many reasons for this, including the fact that, man for man, Labour has had stronger teams. Other reasons have included, first, the complete defeat of the Conservatives in the general intellectual argument and, second, the conviction that, while both parties are broadly agreed about how to run the country, Labour believes more effectively in collectivism—in particular, it can keep the trade unions quieter—than the Conservatives. It has been almost totally accepted that there is no choice between an interventionist and a noninterventionist government, at least partly because the Conservatives have, at most periods, accepted the collectivist thesis. And the defeat of Mr. Heath in February 1974 made it clear that the electorate thought Labour could handle a collectivized economy better than he could. All this goes to prove how thin the shield of Mr. Macmillan's pragmatism was; once it was broken, the Conservative Party lost every natural advantage it had enjoyed for most of the century, particularly its reputation for superiority in the art of government.

The third difficulty Mr. Macmillan faced, especially after 1959, was that of foreign policy. As the Empire diminished, as difficulties at home mounted, and as the terms of world trade shifted to Britain's disadvantage, the consequences of international decline began to be felt, both psychologically and materially. In particular, Britain started to run into balance-of-payments difficulties. Devaluation was unthinkable—the idea of a floating rate was then merely a dream—both because Labour had devalued in 1949 and the Conservatives had used this as proof of their economic incompetence, and because the current rate had become a virility symbol in British politics.

Mr. Macmillan determined on a bold strategy. If his foreign and domestic problems were linked, so he would link their solutions, and he applied to join the European Economic Community. It was questionable then, and is questionable now, whether British membership of the EEC will have the stimulating economic effect advocates of membership have claimed for it, but whatever the merits of entry, a French veto destroyed Mr. Macmillan's hopes and left his government rudderless. Misfortune then rained down on him. With a new Chancellor, Mr. Reginald Maudling, he began to try to spend Britain's way out of her difficulties, and abandoned the financial prudence of Mr. Butler and Mr. Thorneycroft; but balance-of-payments problems continued to worsen, however, and the new leader of the Labour Party, Mr. Harold Wilson, seized these as his principal means of denouncing the myth of Conservative economic competence.

The sorry story of the next few years is briefly told. Mr. Macmillan fell ill and retired. After some bitter infighting he was succeeded by Lord Home, who had to disclaim his peerage to do so. Sir Alec, as he became, had at most a year to rescue the government, and he had no experience or knowledge worth mentioning of domestic or economic matters. He was thus wholly in the hands of Mr. Maudling and the advocates of Mr. Macmillan's inflationary brand of economics; he was also faced, in Mr. Harold Wilson, by a political tactician equal to Mr. Macmillan himself at his best. In the circumstances Sir Alec performed miracles, for when defeat came in 1964 it was by the narrow margin of four parliamentary seats, and the crushing Labour triumph that all had feared did not materialize. Sir Alec was not, however, well rewarded by his party for his efforts, and in 1965 he was replaced by Mr. Edward Heath, who duly and almost inevitably went down to an overwhelming defeat in the general election of 1966. Mr. Heath was to be so important a Conservative leader, and the work he did in opposition was to be of such consequence that it is vital to stress something about his career in Sir Alec's government that those who supported Mr. Heath most warmly between 1965 and 1972 completely forgot: He was on the surface a high spender, and at bottom a managerial collectivist.

Mr. Heath had been the chief whip who repaired the damage done to the Conservative Party by the Suez episode. He was rewarded with the Ministry of Labour, but he held this post for only a few months before becoming, with

Cabinet rank, Britain's negotiator with the EEC. When Sir Alec made him Secretary of State for the Regions and president of the Board of Trade, Mr. Heath became responsible for much of British industry, and also assumed his first major departmental job. During the brief period in which he held this post he showed himself particularly anxious to re-create competition in British industry, and he abolished, in the face of considerable opposition, a number of practices that restricted it. At the same time, he was free with the government's purse, and he spent much on industrial development. The potential contradiction between these two policies was not noticed because he was in office for so brief a period. At the end of that time he appeared to the public as an abrasive individualist: His truer nature appeared to be that of a nonideological manager with an almost incredible grasp of detail.

Thus his nature. But there was something perhaps even more important about Mr. Heath's inner beliefs when he became leader of the party in 1965. Unlike any other Conservative politician of comparable seniority—save, possibly, Mr. Powell—he had read the signs of the fifties more clearly than Mr. Macmillan, with his legerdemain, had allowed anybody else to read them. He saw all the consequences for Britain of a hugely diminished international position, and all the dangers for the Conservative Party of the age of consensus. In spite of the coldness that Mr. Heath projects, it is fair to say that his concern for the decline of his country was more passionate than that of any other major British political figure. When he became leader, therefore, he did not see his task at the head of a defeated party—as Churchill had seen his in 1945—as merely to find some way of tactically coming to terms with an electoral defeat; rather, Mr. Heath saw it as clearly as Churchill had in 1940, as one of saving both party and country.

Mr. Heath set about his task with exemplary managerial thoroughness. Only one Conservative policy—that of entry into the EEC—was sacrosanct. Everything else was to be re-examined and restructured by a complicated network of committees, many of which included anonymous members, experts with no particular sympathy for Conservatism. The object was not merely to look critically at everything the party had stood for since the war, but to produce an election manifesto and a government program so thorough as to be able to overcome the normal shoals and misfortunes that every government meets soon after taking office. Indeed, from the moment Mr. Heath became Prime Minister (in 1970) until 1972, when he reversed his major economic policies, it was common to have a copy of the Conservative manifesto on the table at Cabinet meetings, so that the Prime Minister could cross-examine his colleagues on the progress they were making in the implementation of its provisions.

Withal, the Conservative leadership remained unpopular among members of the party in the country from 1966 until its election victory in 1970. This was normally put down to the coldness of Mr. Heath's personality and the inadequacy of the party's public relations. But in retrospect, it seems possible that it may have had something to do with the method of producing and defending new policies. There is no question but that Mr. Heath produced at least a theoretical revolution in party policy, and broke wholly with the postwar consensus. His government, when it came to power, had a program of radically reducing public expenditure, principally in order to slash taxation and thus reward initiative. Unsuccessful firms were to be penalized by bankruptcy, and only the genuinely weak could look with hope to the welfare state. No part of the program, however, was put across with real vision or power; and its emotional stimulus—Mr. Heath's own vision of the parlous position of the country—which might have justified the harshness and austerity of much of the program seemed unsuccessfully communicated. One must say "seemed," for Mr. Heath, after all, won the 1970 election against all apparent odds, and so came to office with the Conservative Party at last unshackled from the collectivist consensus of 1945–64. A genuine Tory revolutionary, it was thought, had arrived.

There was one important questioning voice. When Mr. Heath became party leader in 1965 he inaugurated a period of debate within the party between the pragmatists—like Mr. Maudling—who were anxious to defend the Macmillan record, attack Labour's mismanagement, and wait to fight another day, and the so-called right-wingers, who were at last enjoying an intellectual renaissance and wanted the Opposition to go wholly for an economic policy based on a commitment to free enterprise and capitalism. Of this conflict the authors of the Nuffield College study *The British General Election of 1970,*[4] Dr. David Butler and Mr. Michael Pinto-Duschinsky, wrote perceptively,

> Although Mr. Heath agreed with the interventionists on the one hand that there was a continuing need for a voluntary incomes policy and, on the other hand, with the free marketeers that individual enterprise was being stifled and industry harmed by "over-government," he had comparatively little interest in their controversies. For he looked to the solution to the problems of the economy in a different direction which can conveniently (if inadequately) be termed "technocratic." Like the advocates of *laissez-faire,* he wished to allow individual enterprise to flourish; but, unlike them, he did not see drastic reductions of governmental activities as the best way of doing this. He saw in structural reforms a way of cutting the area of public interference without significantly reducing the overall level of services provided.

In other words, Mr. Heath's commitment was to a more rigorous form of pragmatism; and only the hunger of a beaten party for a distinctive identity persuaded Conservatives that this was not so. He thus gained the undeserved reputation of a counterrevolutionary.

Nevertheless, and however strong his instinctive pragmatism, Mr. Heath allowed both rhetoric and specific commitments to place him in a trap the way out of which he could not see when his first major crisis came. He most emphatically opposed any explicit form of incomes policy, even after a commitment to incomes policy had become the main trademark of economic fashion.

There was thus, in spite of Mr. Heath's very deep conviction that the nation was in a state of serious crisis, an uncertainty about what was really going to be done. Further, the Conservatives had made a commitment while in opposition to impose new legal restraints on trade union activity, following an unsuccessful attempt (made in pursuit of an incomes policy) to do just that by the Labour government in 1968. Mr. Heath duly passed the legislation necessary for the imposition of these restrictions—very much akin to the disciplines of American law—but, as the event turned out, both the trade union movement and the Labour opposition bitterly opposed what the government had done, and it seems in retrospect that Mr. Heath was tactically unwise in attempting to impose new disciplines on trade unions at the same time as he was beginning to administer an anti-inflationary policy of reduced government spending and sound money; the unions might have been divided and uncertain in their response to any such financial policy, especially when the ministers could effectively argue that rising unemployment was a consequence of excessive wage demands, rather than of the government's general economic policy. In any event, the Conservative Industrial Relations Act provided an instant focus for trade union resistance, which the government proved unable to overcome.

However uncommitted Mr. Heath really was to specific policies—save that of reforming the trade unions and that of British entry into the EEC—the general thrust of his and his government's statement was radical and right-wing; and it was widely believed, among both his friends and his enemies, that he would be ruthless in carrying out the provisions of his manifesto. However, he started to lose time almost at the beginning. Nothing whatever was done in general economic policy until October of 1970; and the public expenditure cuts then made—designed to make it possible to reduce taxation and thus stimulate enterprise—were far from adequate. In the course of 1971, moreover, the government began to come up against very severe political pressures; a number of major British firms, including Rolls-Royce and Upper Clyde Shipbuilders, ran into stormy economic weather. Unemployment began to rise, and the unions neatly tied together their opposition to the Industrial Relations Act and the apparent heartlessness of Conservative policies. As I have already suggested, the modern Conservative Party, because of the fundamental policy decisions it made after 1945, is peculiarly vulnerable to accusations of heartlessness. The party was all the more vulnerable when Mr. Heath began following an unacknowledged incomes policy, in which he strove to ensure that each wage settlement was at least 1 per cent lower than its predecessor. Because of the high degree of state participation in British industry, the government is the country's major employer, and when a government strives to reduce the growth in incomes it almost invariably is drawn into local, individual, and energy-sapping negotiations with the unions. This of course happened to Mr. Heath, and it happened at a time when rising unemployment and workers' militancy had begun to damage the Cabinet's nerve. Perhaps the most extraordinary feature of a retreat that rapidly became a rout was that Mr. Heath and his ministers did not seem to realize that the unemployment levels that eventually forced them to return to a policy of high spending were the delayed results of the extremely tight monetary policy followed by the Labour Chancellor, Mr. Roy Jenkins, before the 1970 election.

When faced with a situation that seemed to be getting out of hand, Mr. Heath pondered the spectrum of consensus and, like Mr. Macmillan, moved to the left. He agreed to subsidize both Rolls-Royce and Upper Clyde, accepted defeat at the hands of the miners in 1972, and passed an Industry Act to provide for huge, and indiscriminate industrial subsidization, a law which broke every rule of monetary restraint he had ever seemed to favor. The worst blow for his erstwhile Conservative followers came, however, during the 1972 parliamentary recess when the Prime Minister, in direct defiance of every vow he had made before the 1970 election, introduced an incomes policy of unbelievable complexity and one that was designed, moreover, to last for all time. Every previous incomes policy, Mr. Wilson's as much as Mr. Macmillan's, was justified as a temporary expedient, designed to meet a crisis; a British Conservative Prime Minister was the first to introduce an essentially collectivist measure of major importance as a permanent feature of government life.

British socialism is, of course, theoretically flawed. Whatever the theoretical commitment to the Marxist creed that flourishes east of the Iron Curtain, the British Labour movement exists in a continual state of tension, because it has two independent parts—the Labour Party and the allied trade union movement. The natural liking of the party for such genuinely socialist instruments as incomes policies clashes with the robber baron principles of trade unionists, who tend to hate incomes policies because their power seems to be reduced by them. It was this confusion within the Labour movement that enabled Mr. Heath to put forward without a great deal of contradiction the idea of a compulsory incomes policy as essentially a responsible and Conservative idea. For a time it seemed as though the mass of the electorate, who generally detest trade unions, would follow him. However, another crisis with the miners arose in 1973, and early in the following year Mr. Heath went to the country and was defeated.

There were probably a host of reasons for his defeat, but the principal one appears to have been the state of dreadful intellectual and moral confusion to which he had reduced his government and his party. All the great ideas of 1970 had been abandoned, and Conservatives did not go into battle—as they had done in that election—convinced that they were standing for something different from socialism. In 1974 Mr. Heath made it clear that he proposed to settle with the miners as soon as he was returned to power; the public reaction to this appeared to be a worried question about the point of asking for a renewed mandate in the first place. Mr. Powell, who decided not to stand in the election, urged a vote for Labour, on the grounds that both parties were socialist in their domestic policies, but only Labour offered the country a chance to get out of Europe. And finally—and I believe this may have been the clinching factor—Labour made it perfectly clear that they were not going to be at war with the trade union movement.

Mr. Heath lost another election in October 1974, and at the beginning of the following year he was deposed from the leadership of his party. He remained, however, a powerful political figure, for reasons that lay essentially in the differences between himself and his successor, Mrs. Margaret Thatcher. Between February and October 1974 Mr. Heath became an ardent coalitionist, thus moving in the fashion of the traditional Tory pragmatist, who seeks office above all, and is not much bothered by ideas. Mrs. Thatcher was a resolute opponent of coalition, for she inclined to favor the abandoned policies of 1970. The idea of coalition is, however, always in favor with a nonideological electorate, and that general feeling, combined with support for the idea from a number of important newspapers, kept Mr. Heath in the public eye. Mr. Heath continued to take the view that rising unemployment, rather than inflation, was the principal problem the country faced, thus holding steadfast to Mr. Macmillan's view in the early sixties and his own in 1971. He dismissed the idea advanced by Sir Keith Joseph that our definitions of full employment state an impossible objective, and that our method of compiling unemployment statistics exaggerates the problem. Mr. Heath further opposed the monetarist view—shared by Sir Keith and Mrs. Thatcher—that Britain faces a choice between a fairly high rate of unemployment now and truly massive unemployment if inflation is not reduced. In summary, all the differences on policy, performance, philosophy, and tactics that have plagued the Conservative Party since the war, and that were for so long concealed from party and country alike by the skill of Mr. Macmillan, re-emerged in their sharpest form ever, and especially in the personalities and attitudes of Mrs. Thatcher and her immediate predecessor.

Over its long history the Conservative Party has seldom been markedly ideological for any long period. But it has had periods of vigorous and sometimes vicious dispute within its own ranks, as well as with opposing parties. The promise of Mr. Macmillan was to take ideology and doctrine altogether outside the area of party policy; and he achieved a respite from intellectual debate largely by adopting most of the maxims of the other side. This might conceivably have worked had not the country itself been in a state of steady decline and had the Conservatives managed to win the general election of 1964. But the decline of a country forces particularly strenuous rethinking in any party that identifies itself as closely with the nation and with government as do the Conservatives. What is perfectly clear from the history of the party in the past thirty years is, first, that the Conservatives must come to terms with what has happened to the country if they are to play a constructive role in its future; second, that however difficult it may be to break with the consensus of the postwar years, this must be done if the British Conservative Party is not to go the way of its Scandinavian counterparts, reduced to impotent rumps following their pragmatic adoption of the nostra of socialism; and third, that the crucial task facing a future Conservative government is to find a way of rolling back the power of the state. It may be that the Tories will be fortunate, and that they will gain power at a time when Labour's performance has so reduced public expectation that it will be easier to undertake monetary contraction and reduced public expenditure measures without creating the kind of outcry and opposition that unmanned Mr. Heath. But even if that happens (and even more if it does not), it will require, in order to implement the Conservative doctrines that alone can prevent Britain from becoming wholly collectivized, both a far greater understanding of policy and a far deeper philosophical commitment than Mr. Heath had in 1970. Of course, it will in any event be exceptionally difficult to change, as Mr. Heath once hoped to, the historical direction of the country, but it is worth making the effort, since there hardly seems much point in political activity designed, as the Conservative defeatists suggested, merely to gain office at the head of a socialist state. What Churchill once called the long, drawling tides of drift and surrender have been gaining force in the Conservative Party for a generation; it is with them that the party has failed to cope, and the next chance may well be its last.

The Economic Tensions of British Democracy

Samuel Brittan

There is nothing uniquely British in the economic and other tensions that have produced the present strains in the political system of a country that was once a model for democracy in the rest of the world. They arise instead from weaknesses endemic to liberal representative democracies everywhere, but the pressures—material, institutional, and ideological—have been more severe in Britain; hence the label "English sickness" when they turn up elsewhere. I shall start off with the material pressures, move on to elaborate a hypothesis about democratic crisis, and conclude with the ideological factors that have made Britain's difficulties especially severe and that would need to change before we can hope for a lasting improvement.

The most widely discussed economic problems in the United Kingdom are the same as in the United States or in most other Western countries. The rate of inflation has been increasing from one economic cycle to the next. Yet at the same time, the average rate of unemployment in each cycle, measured by conventional statistics, has also risen. For instance, the unemployment rate reached at the *peak* of the 1973 boom was the same as that reached in the *trough* of the 1958 recession, a departure from the politicians' view of a constant "trade-off" between unemployment and inflation. Unemployment is now in the 1–1.5 million range not seen in the United Kingdom since before World War II. Yet the most the government can hope is to reduce inflation from its 1975 peak of 30 per cent to around 10 per cent by, say, 1978; and it is anyone's guess when it will start accelerating in the next cycle.

The monetary and employment difficulties common to Western countries have been aggravated by weaknesses in grass-roots productive performance that *do* seem special to the United Kingdom. Although until recently wages were growing no more quickly in Britain than in other countries, productivity was rising a good deal more slowly. In the period since 1960, real output per head grew by just over 2 per cent annually, compared with productivity growth in Germany of nearly 4 per cent, French growth of about 5 per cent, and Japanese growth of nearly 10 per cent. The only major country to show a similar output performance in this period was the United States, which started from a much higher absolute level and even then produced an annual per capita growth rate of nearly 3 per cent.

A symptom, which many have mistaken for a cause, has been the succession of balance-of-payments crises and currency depreciations. The pound was devalued in 1949 and 1967; and in the four years after it floated in 1972, it suffered a depreciation of more than 40 per cent against the average of other currencies.

As a result of this combination of weaknesses, Britain was particularly badly placed to meet the international crisis caused by the fivefold rise in oil prices at a time of very rapid world inflation. The miners' strike in February 1974, which led to a three-day week in British industry and to the second humiliating defeat of the Heath Conservative government by the National Union of Mineworkers in two years, had a traumatic effect on the public mood. When the Chancellor of the Exchequer, Mr. Denis Healey, said in his budget speech of November 1974 that most people could expect no increase in their standard of living "at least in the new few years," the main reservation among commentators was on whether this prognosis was too optimistic.

These events have been met neither with Churchillian vision and leadership nor with the national tradition of "muddling through." Instead, there has been an underlying doubt about the ability of the governmental system to cope. Both class and political tensions were greater in the early 1970s than at any time within living memory. The power of the unions in national politics and the hostility that this generates among their opponents are unparalleled since the general strike of 1926. The pragmatic politics of the 1950s and 1960s has been succeeded by a renewed verbal battle between collectivism and capitalism; and the inflation of 1974–75 unleashed a ferocious struggle over the division of the national cake both before and after taxes.

The resulting anxiety about the future is not confined to politicians, officials, academics, and journalists. A National Opinion Poll, specially commissioned for the BBC "Panorama" television program in September 1974, showed that 65 per cent of the respondents thought that there was a threat to democracy. At least 60–80 per cent of the respondents mentioned rising prices, "the power of the trade unions," and "the growth of private armies" as specific threats.

Two endemic threats to liberal representative democracy are:

1. the generation of excessive expectations; and
2. the disruptive effects of the pursuit of group self-interest in the marketplace.

These two threats are, in an obvious sense of the word, "economic." I do not wish to underplay other kinds of threat, such as those arising from the clash of irreconcilable nationalisms or from other manifestations of the herd impulse and the self-destructive impulse, of which the troubles of Northern Ireland are such an obvious example. The diagnosis of non-economic threats serves—unfortunately—to strengthen my argument.

The simplified but realistic view of representative democracy applied here is that politicians compete in the political marketplace for the votes of an extensive electorate in the same way that oilmen bid for oil or salesmen bid for customers. The principles or policies supported by a political party may be important for its success at a given moment; however, they have no deeper or more permanent significance than the brand lines that a department store carries this month but may well wish to change next spring or autumn. This model appears particularly relevant to the United Kingdom, where governments have been notable for spectacular "U turns" in policy. To take just one example, the Heath government of 1970–74 committed itself not to impose a statutory incomes policy; yet it left office after losing an election in which it was "seeking a mandate" for the statutory incomes policy that it had operated for the previous sixteen months.

The generation of excessive expectations follows from the competitive nature of democracy, combined with the irrationality of the individual elector's spending much time or trouble informing himself. For most people the great political issues are "subhobbies" to which they devote less attention than to bridge; and there is little check either on dark urges or on bursts of generalized indignation. The modern "economic" analysis of rational political behavior has highlighted the *voting paradox,* that is, the problem of finding a self-interested motive for voting when the probability of any one vote determining the outcome is vanishingly small. If a self-interested citizen has little or no incentive to vote, he has even less incentive to make a detailed study of facts, controversies, and policies. That relatively minor factors can affect an elector's decision is suggested by protests sometimes made by British Labour Party leaders, who are most threatened by voter abstention, against the possible appearance on polling night of popular television serials.

Lack of information in itself would merely cause electors to favor the wrong party in particular elections or to support isolated wrong decisions. The more basic trouble is that the lack of a budget constraint among voters gives these errors a particular bias. In their own private lives, people know that more of one thing means less of something else, on a given income and capital. In the absence of such knowledge in the political sphere, electorates tend to expect too much from government action at too little cost —for example, a painless improvement in economic growth or reduction in inflation; and they tend both to praise and to blame governments for things that are largely outside government control. The impetus to consistency, without the discipline and responsibility of personal experience, is not strong.

The temptation to encourage false expectations among the electorate thus becomes overwhelming to politicians. The opposition parties are bound to promise to do better, and the government party must join in the auction— explaining away the past and outbidding its rivals for the future, whether by general hints or detailed promises. Within each party, moreover, the normal competitive processes tend to elevate leaders who genuinely believe that they can improve the tradeoffs among policies more than is actually possible—usually by some form of minor improvement in machinery or administration. The obvious British examples were Harold Wilson and Edward Heath, both of whom attached disproportionate weight to Whitehall reorganization, not only in their initial plans while in opposition but also in their first years of power. Such attitudes are perfectly compatible with a great deal of apparent tough talking, but they do not suit the skeptic or realist who actually knows the score.

There are, of course, periods of masochistic reaction in which parties vie with each other to promise hard times ahead. The period since the 1973 oil crisis is just such an episode. But closer inspection shows a large element of either hypocrisy or self-deception; for although the politicians hesitate to promise a larger cake, competition continues on promises about the distribution of the cake.

The behavior of politicians during 1974 was a good example of the political auction during such a masochistic period. Although it called for "sacrifices" because of inflation and the oil crisis, the Labour government froze the rents of council tenants, from whom it expected to draw a large vote, while the Conservative opposition promised to reduce the interest payments on mortgages "by Christmas," at a time of rapidly rising prices.

This is not, of course, a complete theory of political expectations, which are determined by innumerable forces apart from competitive vote-bidding. The spread of information about other people's life styles through the media and advertising, so that they look like attainable ideals rather than fantasies, is frequently cited. The breakdown of traditional ideas of hierarchy, to be discussed below, is another obvious influence. It has also been suggested that expectations tend to be low during protracted periods of economic hardship, as they were in the depression of the 1930s. The gap between expectation and reality is greater during periods of prosperity and advance, and perhaps greatest of all when expectations are frustrated by a sudden and unexpected check to progress. The main point to stress is that democracy, viewed as a process of political competition, itself imparts a systematic upward bias to expectations and compounds the other influences at work. What has gone is the tacit belief in limiting the role of political decision; and this is likely to put a burden on democratic procedures that they are not designed to bear.

The disruptive effects of the pursuit of group self-interest in the marketplace follows from elementary economic logic. The most obvious form of this is the conflict of different groups of trade unionists—ostensibly with the government or employers, but in reality with each other—for shares of the national product. This rivalry induces more and more sections of the population, including those who had previously relied on individual efforts, to adopt militant trade unionist attitudes in self-defense. Among groups who have behaved in this way in recent years have been traditionally moderate workers such as bank employees and civil servants, who claim that they are forced to behave like the more traditionally militant groups to protect their relative shares.

The real danger of such action is that there is no equivalent in the sphere of organized group conflict to Adam Smith's "invisible hand," which harmonizes, however imperfectly, the individual pursuit of self-interest with the general interest. There is nothing to prevent the rivalry of coercive groups from reaching a stage where nonnegotiable claims add up to more than the total national product.

Union monopolies, moreover, differ in an important way from other organized groups. A business monopoly, or cartel with market power, will hold its output below competitive levels for the sake of higher prices. A farmer's association will try to achieve the same effect by political lobbying. But none of these will normally withdraw output from the market until representatives of the public sign an agreement to pay more. This is a quasi-political power or threat, different in many ways from the textbook monopoly. Of course, there have been collective boycotts and even a resort to violence in business history, especially in the United States in the late nineteenth century, but nothing as extended in scale or as pervasive throughout the economy as the effects of union power in the context of the commitment to full employment that prevailed in the United Kindom for most of the postwar period.

It is important not to make the wrong case against the strike threat system. A wage increase granted to a group of workers with some degree of monopoly power, such as the coal miners in the United Kingdom, does not automatically lead to continuing inflation, as the Galbraithians believe. Inflation is produced by governments trying to buy time and to paper over conflicts.

If the government did not react to the wage increase by adapting its fiscal and money supply policies (including the subsidy that it gives to the National Coal Board), the first-round effects would be (1) to put up the price of coal, hence reducing the amount sold and putting some miners out of work, and (2) possibly to reduce expenditure on goods other than coal, thus putting other workers out of a job too.

In the long run the miners' wage increase would cause the relative wages of workers in other industries to fall by an equivalent amount, with rises in employment in these other industries to compensate for the fall in employment in mining. In this case, the duration of the long run can vary and depends on how quickly workers in other industries would allow their wage relativities to fall. But it is unlikely to be much less than the length of time until the next election, causing politicians to be more preoccupied with the first-round effects of the policy than with the long-run effects.

Inflation comes into the picture when the government expands the money supply and increases its expenditure in an attempt to mop up the initial unemployment by pushing more spending power into the economy. But this, of its nature, can only be of temporary assistance—since demand is increased throughout the economy, raising prices and reducing the value of the initial wage increase given to the miners. The miners are unlikely to be fooled indefinitely by "money illusion," and they will demand and receive further wage increases to restore the real incomes that their original settlements were intended to achieve. This in turn will threaten unemployment and tempt or force governments into a further expansion of monetary demand and a repetition of the earlier process.

As the spiral proceeds, the result is not inflation but accelerating inflation. In the last analysis, the authorities have to choose between accepting an indefinite increase in the rate of inflation, abandoning full employment to the extent necessary to break the collective wage-push power of the unions, and tackling the unions directly, which most politicians think would require a degree of coercion incompatible with a liberal system of government.

The increased levels of unemployment in Britain (which also reflect influences such as social security payments) suggest some halfhearted government resistance to the acceleration of inflation, but insufficient resistance to stop it permanently. The failure of the two attempts to reform the collective bargaining system, the 1968 "In Place of Strife" proposals of Mrs. Barbara Castle and the 1971 Industrial Relations Act of Mr. Heath's government, and the successive breakdowns in incomes policies demonstrate the continuing impotence of British governments in face of the union threat.

The basic problem is that the benefits from restraint in the use of group market power are what economists call "public goods." They consist of things such as fuller employment or faster economic growth (or, indirectly, price stabilization) that are thinly diffused among the whole population, while the costs are incurred by the group that exercises restraint. It is therefore in the interests of each union group that other unions should show restraint while it exploits its own monopoly power. If the leadership of a union is prepared to look beyond the (fairly short-term) self-interest of its own members, it is likely to be thrown out of office. One does not have to look for "Reds under the bed." The "militant moderates" will do the job, and rationally so from the members' point of view.

As the above examples show, the two threats to democracy—excessive expectations and the generation of group self-interest—are linked. They both place an excessive burden on what Bertrand de Jouvenel has called the "sharing-out function of government"—the activities of the government in distributing resources through its tax and spending policies, and its direct intervention in the marketplace.

Some indication of this burden is the massive excess of government spending over revenue, running in 1975 at a good 10 per cent of the national product. Equally, the range of activities in which the government has been forced to intervene directly has grown rapidly: The 1975 Industry Act is but one well-publicized example of the government obtaining powers for intervening in business decision-making, and in operating businesses itself. The last decade is littered with "lame duck" enterprises, such as Rolls-Royce and British Leyland, which governments of both parties have been pressed to preserve, whatever the underlying viability of the business concerned. An even more important sharing-out function is the obligation that governments have had under recent incomes policies to take a view on wages of different groups, ranging from the Heath government's stress on "fair relativities" to Mr. Wilson's attempt to narrow differentials by means of the £6 per head limit to wage increases imposed in August 1975.

There have been many warnings about the destructive tendencies of democracy, dating back well into the nineteenth century. Bagehot's Introduction to the Second Edition of *The English Constitution,* written after the 1867 Reform Bill, is full of gloomy forebodings about the effects of enfranchising an ignorant and greedy electorate, and historian J. A. Froude made similar comments in 1887 following the Third Reform Bill. Why then, if these threats and tensions are endemic to liberal representative democracy, are they beginning to surface only now?

The view of democracy I have been expounding derives from the writings of Austrian-American economist Joseph Schumpeter.* His chapter on the subject is prescribed reading in many U.S. college courses; but the emphasis tends to be on the normal healthy working of the competitive political market rather than on the author's warnings and forebodings. Schumpeter himself made it clear that democracy would not work satisfactorily unless certain constraints were observed. These included:

1. Some constraint on the effective range of political decision-making.
2. Political self-restraint among the electorate.
3. The existence of an independent, powerful, and well-trained bureaucracy.

The third condition is necessary because politicians are specialists in winning elections rather than in policy planning or administration. The existence of this bureaucracy could, for a long time, be taken for granted in the United Kingdom. But the extension of government activity has led to many new agencies dealing with areas such as industrial policy, wages and profits, or publicity, staffed from outside the traditional civil service. The scope for patronage has been so much extended that there are at least as many "jobs

* *Capitalism, Socialism and Democracy* (4th posthumous ed., 1952).

for the boys" in Britain as elsewhere. Moreover, the old-fashioned mandarins—who were often infuriatingly fuddy-duddy, but did put a brake on the despotic ambitions of politicians who achieved a bare plurality—are being replaced by a more up-to-date, compliant breed.

Nevertheless, the main erosion has been in the other two constraints—a limited range for political decision and self-restraint by the electorate. The last decade has seen the encroachment of political decision-making into many fields in the United Kingdom. Governments have in recent years attempted to intervene in judicial processes, for example to remove the disqualifications imposed by courts of law upon the Clay Cross councilors who failed to obey laws about expenditure on housing, and more frequently in economic processes. For about nine of the years since 1965, government has controlled prices and incomes in some way or other, and since 1972 there has been government control of profits as well. In 1974, subsidies on a wide range of foods were announced, as was a policy to "stabilize the prices of certain items in a shopping basket," such as particular cuts of meat. Free negotiation between buyers and sellers has been further affected by a series of complex consumer laws.

Of great importance too have been government measures to provide particular goods, services, or incomes to favored groups at subsidized levels. A particular example of this is in housing, where the government has intervened to build houses to rent at prices that often do not cover the collection costs, or to provide special tax concessions on loans to those buying their own houses. Similarly, large subsidies have been provided to state-owned industries to prevent price increases, pay higher wages, or prevent unemployment. When Upper Clyde Shipbuilders found itself unable to meet its financial obligations in 1972, a workers' sit-in combined with a well-orchestrated publicity campaign persuaded the government to provide further financial assistance. A similar tactic forced the government to back a "workers'" co-operative producing motorcycles at Meriden in 1974, although the profit potential was so low that the Department of Industry's own investigators reported that the project was not economically viable. Many other instances exemplify the extension of political decision-making.

The decline of political self-restraint among the electorate has been both a cause and a product of the rise in government intervention. When only a few groups, such as farmers or the old, are clearly favored by political intervention it is relatively easy for other people to maintain a dignified aloofness. But when intervention is across the board, it becomes clear that such aloofness is causing a significant decline in one's share of the national cake. This can be seen in the rise of militant trade unionism already cited among those, particularly white-collar groups, who in earlier periods had relied on individualist efforts.

Mass electorates were able to accept the Schumpeter condition of self-restraint for a surprisingly long period partly because they were slow to realize their power. The lack of incentives for the voter to inform himself has already been emphasized. There was also a series of ad hoc events like the First World War, which produced an external threat and a patriotic myth to override sectional conflicts, and the Great Depression, which weakened the market power of the trade unions.

But just as important was an ethic that took a long time to erode, an ethic that limited the demands on the sharing-out functions of the state. As Irving Kristol has emphasized,† personal success was seen by nineteenth-century defenders of capitalism as having a firm connection with

† *Capitalism Today,* Chap. 2, ed. Bell and Kristol (New York: Mentor Books, 1971).

"duty performed." In a society "still permeated by a Puritan ethic" it "was agreed that there was a strong correlation between certain personal virtues—frugality, industry, sobriety, reliability, piety—and the way in which power, privilege, and property were distributed. And this correlation was taken to be the sign of a just society, not merely a free one. Samuel Smiles or Horatio Alger would have regarded Professor Hayek's writings [divorcing reward from merit] as slanderous of his fellow Christians, blasphemous of God, and ultimately subversive of the social order."

The point that Kristol does not bring out sufficiently is that the public morality of early capitalist bourgeois society was a transitional one. On its own grounds it could not hope to stand up to serious analysis. Luck was even then as important as merit in the gaining of awards, and merit was inherently a subjective concept in the eye of the beholder. Early capitalist civilization was living on the moral heritage of the feudal system under which each man had a superior to whom he owed obligations and from whom he received protection in a "great chain of duties." A medieval king was expected to "do justice and to render each his due." It was not a matter of what the king thought a subject ought to have, or what the subject thought best for himself, but what belonged to him according to custom, which in turn was supported by theological sanction.

For a long time capitalist civilization was able to live on this feudal legacy, and the aura of legitimacy was transferred from the feudal lord to the employer, from the medieval hierarchy of position to that derived from the luck of the marketplace. But this feudal legacy was bound to be extinguished by the torchlight of secular and rationalistic inquiry, which was itself so closely associated with the rise of capitalism. The personal qualities of middle-class leaders did not help to kindle that affection for the social order that is probably necessary if it is not to be blamed for the inevitable tribulations and disappointments of most people's lives. Modern politicians and business chiefs lack the glamor of an aristocracy. With neither the trappings of tradition, nor the heroic qualities of great war leaders or generals, they cannot excite the identification or hero worship that previously reconciled people to much greater differences of wealth and position than exist today. Moreover, the "fairer" the process of selection, the less the governing classes are differentiated by special clothes or accents, the more they will be resented. At most they are tolerated on the strict condition that they bring results; and we have seen that expectations here tend to be excessive.

Schumpeter himself had some halfhearted hopes that the degree of institutional consensus and agreement on fundamentals required for the working of democracy might be restored under "socialism." For one thing, the issue of capitalism *vs.* socialism would be out of the way, and there would be no more argument about profits, dividends, private ownership of capital, or gains from rising land values. Moreover, the twentieth-century development of nonpolitical agencies made socialism possible and perhaps compatible with democracy. By "socialism" he had in mind the old-fashioned definition of collective control over the means of production. But the condition of success was that democratic politics *not* extend to economic affairs. Beyond setting the rules in the most general way possible, it was essential that politicians resist the temptation to interfere with the activities of the managers of state enterprises and regulatory boards. Indeed, Schumpeter remarked that at long last managers would be able to do their jobs without guilt feelings and with more freedom not only from interfering politicians but also from fussing committees of consumers, demands for workers' control, and all other demands for "participation."

We do not, however, need to follow out these paradoxes,

because the type of collectivism now in vogue among all parties concerns not only ownership of productive assets but also—and more important—relative incomes. The popular desire is to transfer from the private to the public sphere the determination of who gets how much, and to base this determination neither on market values, nor on egalitarian principles, nor on some compromise between them, but by a revival of the medieval notion of the just wage—a doctrine sometimes miscalled "fairness." This is to be done, moreover, without benefit of the feudal relationships and scholastic theology that enabled an earlier age to attach a meaning to such concepts. These demands risk straining liberal democracy to the breaking point.

These intellectual influences just discussed, are, of course, in operation in most Western countries. But the United Kingdom does stand out in the extent of its obsession with interpersonal and intergroup comparisons. This is seen in concepts such as "relative deprivation" in sociology, "inequality" (a loaded way of describing differences) and "interdependent utilities" in economics, and "equal freedom" in political philosophy. Much of this ideology and its accompanying jargon originate with American academics. But it has a much greater hold in British than in American public life, and it permeates the media. The main contribution of the English intelligentsia is to focus all attention on relativities to the exclusion of absolutes. Moreover, their object in so doing is not to stir up personal rivalry and emulation, which add to the interests and joys, as well as the unhappiness of life; it is instead to emphasize differences while asserting that they should not be there. The result is to reinforce the type of envious, self-defeating attitudes revealed by the United Kingdom Survey Research Unit, in which 80 per cent of those questioned said they would rather receive an extra £4 a week in common with everyone else than receive an extra £5, if everyone else's income were to rise by the still higher sum of £6.

If comparisons are always with other people, and never with past achievements, then the hope of progress is at an end; and what the pessimistic theologians have failed to do will have been achieved by the secular egalitarians. If we look at definite things, such as treatment of children, the levels of nutrition, health, and housing enjoyed by the poorest, or the efficiency and humanity of the penal system, improvement is possible. In the realm of intangibles, such as self-respect and regard for others, improvement is more difficult, but can still be envisaged; and this also applies to the reduction of coercion in human affairs. But if all that matters is whether other people are better or worse off than oneself in these respects, then human history is a zero-sum game. Even if the principle of diminishing marginal utility is misapplied to assert that the gains of those who move up are greater than the losses of those who move down, then all advance stops when equality has been reached; what is more the definition of equality is far from obvious and likely to cause extreme acrimony, with most people feeling that they have been treated less equally than others.

These difficulties aside, there is no reason to suppose that any target reduction in "inequality" (or even in the share of property income) would supply a basis for consent to the social or economic structure. Indeed, the more that policy concentrates on eliminating disparities and differentials, the more outrageous remaining inequalities will seem. Moreover, the smaller the financial contrast between the mass of wage and salary earners and the wealthy minority, the greater the attention that is likely to be paid to relativities among workers. As it is 90 per cent of Britain's consumer spending comes from wages, salaries, and social security payments, and the annual wage round is to a large extent a contest among different groups of workers for relative shares. It is one of the defects of the present preoccupation with differentials, whether from a desire to establish an "incomes policy" or form a wish to iron out "inequality," that each group becomes much more keenly aware of what other groups are obtaining and much more critical of the basis of comparison. Comparisons can always be made in more than one way, and this fact increases rather than diminishes the ferocity of the struggle.

The ideal of equality has had a noble role in human history. It has served to assert that all men and women are entitled to respect, and to rally people against oppression. But it has now turned sour, and it has done immense damage to my country. Liberal democracy will not be saved by detailed policy programs that will soon be overtaken by events. It could yet be saved if contemporary egalitarianism were to lose its hold over the intelligentsia. But this will only happen if those who recognize it for the disease it has become are prepared to come out in the open and have uncongenial labels placed upon them. The disease is a general one rather than an "English sickness." It has simply progressed further in Britain than in the United States or in Continental Europe.

Welfare in the Welfare State

Leslie Lenkowsky

The welfare state is, in a sense, a British invention. Although social insurance originated in Imperial Germany, the goals and methods adopted elsewhere were more likely to be those of Edwardian England. To careful observers such as Lord Bryce, New Zealand seemed "the social laboratory of the world," but the research and writings of British social reformers have had the wider influence. The Scandinavian nations proved more able to fashion durable social reforms out of the economic slump of the 1920s and 1930s; yet it was the wartime plan of Sir William Beveridge that captured the imagination of the world. Indeed, the term "welfare state" first came into widespread usage to denote the postwar programs for social security and health care established by the Labour government in Great Britain.

A generation later, one might well wonder whether the bill for this burst of national ingenuity has at last come due. Is the price of leadership in providing "cradle to grave" security a steady decline in economic vitality, of which the current crisis is the latest and more severe instance? Has the "namby-pamby state," to use Andrew Shonfield's term, turned Britain into a country of deadbeats, "floating through life on a kind of giant mattress provided by the state, consisting of a combination of cottonwool and old-fashioned down"?[1] Was Beatrice Webb right to object to the wave of Liberal reforms that culminated with the establishment of unemployment and sickness insurance in 1911 and 1912?—because, as she later wrote:

> The fact that sick and unemployed persons were entitled to money incomes without any corresponding obligation to get well and keep well, or to seek and keep employment, seemed to us likely to encourage malingering and a disinclination to work for their livelihood.[2]

Would it not be ironic if the germs of the "English sickness" were to be found in the National Health Service and its kindred enterprises?

During the relative affluence of the 1950s and early 1960s, it would have been ridiculous to think so. There was a great debate then over reforming the welfare state, but the critics addressed themselves to entirely different concerns. To some Conservatives and a few liberal economists, the continuing expense of the health and social services was simply unnecessary. They argued that, contrary to Beveridge's assumption of high postwar unemployment, the average Briton was prosperous enough to pay directly for whatever help he needed, and that the resulting competition among providers would improve its quality. The Fabians and some Socialists saw an increasingly affluent Britain becoming an "irresponsible society" by failing to give a larger share of a bigger pie to those most in need. And some of the country's fiscal and monetary policy experts, recognizing that sustained economic growth was far from assured, worried about the welfare state's claim on aggregate demand. Few souls troubled about its impact on individual initiative and self-reliance.

But even economists were hard-pressed to explain Britain's calamitous record in the 1970s, and so, once again, there was a revival of interest in the pampering theory. A key plank of Margaret Thatcher's platform was her claim that the welfare state has mollycoddled the nation and given rise to a "progressive consensus" that scoffs at self-help and hard work. The support for these views by Sir Keith Joseph, who had presided over the health and social services during the administration of Edward Heath, endowed them with the credibility of a penitent. With its proposed "new industrial strategy," the Wilson-Callaghan Labour government moved in a similar direction, promising to give lower priority to social programs and higher to identifying and supporting manufacturing firms likely to grow. "Productivity" became a fashionable word among economic planners. A Downing Street "think tank" report on the automobile industry, for example, reported, "With the same power at his elbow, and doing the same job, a continental car worker normally produces twice as much as his British counterpart."[3] The report blamed overmanning, restrictive work rules, low investment, and similar industrial conditions for British sluggishness. Yet these alone may not be sufficient to explain how the nation, conserving energy by a three-day work week in the winter of 1974, could still manage to produce nearly four days of output; many observers suggested that, except in emergencies, British workers have simply become lazy.

Such evidence as can be gathered, however, does not easily fit the notion that the welfare state has contributed to Britain's plight by reducing the incentives to work harder. For one thing, other countries have devoted as much or more of their resources to welfare programs without sharing Britain's economic weakness. For another, the growth of Britain's welfare state has not stopped private spending from increasing throughout most of the postwar era. And in the presumably central matter of income redistribution, the impact of the British welfare state has so far been rather mild. What the welfare state has done is expand in such a way that the services sector of the British economy has grown much faster than the manufacturing and industrial sector; the welfare state has hurt Britain not so much by dampening its energies as by channeling them into less productive endeavors.

THE WELFARE STATES

Except in its health service, Beveridge observed at the beginning of his 1942 report, "British provision for security, in adequacy of amount and in comprehensiveness, will stand comparison with that of any other country; few countries will stand comparison with Britain."[4] Thirty years after the adoption of his major proposals, the reverse is more nearly the case. Among comparable nations, Britain's welfare provisions are apt to seem relatively stingy. If there is an exception, it is health care, where the comprehensiveness of the National Health Service (if not its adequacy) usually exceeds that of medical arrangements elsewhere. In social programs as well as in economic growth, Britain now finds its European compeers in the two least industrialized nations, Italy and Ireland.

One measure of this change is the proportion of money allocated to the welfare state. In 1972 (one of the last years of "normalcy"), Britain used 22 per cent of its national income for social security and medical care. Except for Ireland, every member of the Common Market devoted a higher proportion of its income for such uses, with Germany leading the way at 29 per cent.[5] Only Italy and Ireland spent less per capita for social programs.[6] Even the United States, not usually pictured as generous in these areas, devoted 14 per cent of its national product to public expenditures for health and welfare programs.[7] Adding private spending would bring the total still closer to the proportion used by the one-time "exemplar" of the welfare state.

Nor has Britain been notably liberal in particular programs that might be thought to "pamper" its citizens. Its pensions for disabled workers amount to less than half the earnings of average industrial employees; so do its benefits given in sick pay. Again, save Ireland, the other EEC countries do better. Indeed, if any nation encouraged malingering, it would be Germany, which replaces more than 90 per cent of the wages lost due to illness.[8] A person out of work in Britain could expect to receive no more than 85 per cent of his normal weekly salary in unemployment pay; in France, Denmark, and the Netherlands, he is apt to receive no less.[9] Even the initial advantages of the National Health Service compared with medical care elsewhere have steadily diminished. The maligned American health care system has, in fact, been growing *more* rapidly.[10]

Of course, international comparisons such as these can be misleading. Countries may face different social conditions and have different objectives for social policy. Public assistance in Britain, for example, has been among the most generous in Europe; benefit levels are higher, and eligibility requirements are less stringent. The reason is that British social insurance has sought to provide a minimum pension for all. Since the same benefits go to those with other resources and those without, they have typically lagged behind rising standards of living. As a result, in 1970, more than a quarter of the nation's elderly obtained supplementary assistance, and another 15 per cent were thought to be eligible but not claiming. In contrast, only 3 per cent of Germany's old people were on relief.[11] An insurance plan geared to maintaining preretirement earnings, combined with a dynamic economy, provided pensions that could prevent destitution in old age. Though the cost of the

German scheme would be higher, its impact on self-reliance might well be less pronounced.

Countries also differ in how they pay for these programs. Through social security contributions, the British taxpayer in 1973 supplied only 16.3 per cent of total revenues. American taxpayers raised 24 per cent of public receipts in this fashion, while the proportion in some of the European countries was even higher, reaching nearly 40 per cent in France and the Netherlands.[12] More than any other Common Market member except Denmark, Britain disperses the cost of the welfare state by charging it to general levies, such as income, sales, and corporate taxes. As a result, the penalties for making too many visits to the doctor or for prolonging sick leave are felt indirectly, if at all. The temptation to malinger is obvious, though whether or not any other arrangement can effectively control demand for these programs is an open issue.

Perhaps the main conclusion to be drawn from this comparison is that the relationship between the welfare state and economic vitality is a complex one. Some countries, like Germany, are both generous and prosperous. Others, like Ireland, have managed to be neither. Britain falls in between, though it is tending toward Ireland in both attributes. It may be that self-reliance and social programs are mutually reinforcing, although the simpler explanation is that the forces affecting national dynamism are broader than a particular set of welfare policies. Insofar as pampering has affected growth, the important matter would seem to be not the scope of the welfare state, but rather, how it operates.

THE PERSPECTIVE FROM BRITAIN

In virtually all the major industrialized nations, political debates about the welfare state have raged during the seventies. In the French elections of 1973 and 1974, "social welfare vs. growth" was a main point of contention between Gaullists and Socialists. In Denmark, where the welfare state is financed mostly by general revenues, an antitax party became the second-largest bloc in parliament in 1973. The Swedes, reportedly, have become concerned about the price in personal freedom extracted in return for Europe's most extensive social programs.[13] Germany and Belgium have undertaken major efforts to overhaul their social security systems, as has distant New Zealand. And in the United States, welfare reform—in one or another meaning of the term—has been high on the national agenda since 1968.

In short, whether stingy or moderate by international standards, social policy may still look rampantly profligate at home. And perhaps with good reason. Why, after all, should Britain spend as much of its national income on social programs as, say, Germany does? A lesser amount could, conceivably, purchase as much "welfare" as a higher sum would in a different country. By the same token, the smaller figure could even be too much for a particular nation to bear without harming its potential for economic growth. Regardless of the scope of social programs elsewhere, a country might still be pampering its citizens more than it should.

Is this the case in Britain? Because of its early leadership among welfare states, might Britain have aspired to preserve a stature it could neither afford nor attain? And in so doing, has it created the conditions of economic decline? The evidence suggests not.

There is no question that welfare spending in Britain has increased prodigiously during the last two decades. Between 1953 and 1973, public expenditures at constant prices rose by 506 per cent for the social services, 275 per cent for education, 159 per cent for social security, and 141 per cent for the health service.[14] Not all of this growth was controllable. A longer life span inevitably means that more money is needed for pensions, just as a bigger school-age population requires extra amounts for teachers, classrooms, and the like. Particularly in education, some of the increase was a consequence of underinvestment in the period between the wars. Still, both Conservative and Labour governments have also made deliberate efforts to expand the welfare state. The vast rise in public expenditures testifies to Harold Macmillan's commitment to a home-owning democracy, Harold Wilson's to a university-trained technocracy, and both parties' to a well-fed gerontocracy.

But as Rudolf Klein has observed, the real handmaiden of public spending has been prosperity, not political ideology.[15] Over most of the last two decades, the British economy has been growing, sometimes in fits and starts, but nonetheless at an annual rate only slightly below 3 per cent. Despite the huge increase in social spending, public expenditure on goods and services went only from 29 to 31 per cent of the gross national product, while the increase in income transfers had similar proportions.[16] Offsetting the expansion of the welfare state was the contraction of the garrison one; from 25 per cent of the budget in 1953, defense outlays fell to 10 per cent in 1973.[17] This, together with the nation's brief periods of affluence, lessened the financial burden of a generous social policy.

To be sure, the combination did not leave much room for reducing taxation. On the contrary, in growing slightly faster than the economy as a whole, the welfare state pre-empted a larger share of each year's new resources. By 1970, more than 40 per cent of the gross national product was being taken in taxes, the second highest ratio in the Common Market.[18] In personal income and national insurance taxes alone, the share rose from 12.7 per cent of total income in 1963 to 17.1 per cent in 1970, before declining to 16.1 per cent in 1973. The average male employee usually did not have to pay direct taxes before World War II, but by 1963, 8.8 per cent of his income was taken in taxes and a decade later, a swingeing 21.1 per cent.[19] What was not purchased by raising new revenues was, of course, eventually paid for by an inflated currency.

Yet remarkably, the living standards of most Britons suffered only modestly, if that. The average wage-earner paid more in taxes because he had become prosperous enough to enter the higher tax brackets. Except for the recession year of 1962, not until 1974 was there a year in which the net real income of the typical Briton declined; previously, it had grown at an annual rate of 2 per cent or more (though from 1964 to 1969, under the Labour government, the annual increase averaged 1 per cent).[20] As the welfare state expanded, disposable income shrank from 74 per cent of the gross national product to 69 per cent. Likewise, consumption fell from 73 per cent to 63 per cent, although part of this reflected a major rise in personal savings during the 1950s.[21] But rising personal prosperity was evident both in the vastly increased ownership of goods, like televisions, refrigerators, and washing machines, and in a flourishing private sector, even in areas of social spending. Though public housing drove many landlords out of business, the proportion of British families who lived in their own homes went from 29 per cent in 1950 to 52 per cent in 1973.[22] Private health insurance, particularly in group plans, has been expanding rapidly, and although the number is declining, nearly half of all medical specialists still have a part-time practice of their own.[23] Half of the British work force participates in occupational pension plans, which have become a major source of new investment capital.[24] Perhaps most surprising, private charities, instead of disappearing in the face of so much public benevolence, have altered and enlarged their role.[25]

Undeniably, less social spending and more consumption would have made for a more desirable economic policy. The average Briton, at least, would have obtained a larger share of the country's prosperity. Between 1964 and 1967, *The Economist* estimates, government took 85 per cent of the new growth, leaving little incentive for improving productivity.[26] But this was not a typical period, for since the end of the war the average Briton has not done that badly. In any event, there is no evidence that he strongly opposed using more national resources for social purposes or that he obtained no benefits from increased social spending. Whether he would have done still better with a smaller welfare state depends upon what other means (if any) would have been used to perform the same tasks.

Thus the real problem of British social spending is not that it expanded too quickly while the nation grew, but that it continues to expand while the economy has all but stopped. Between 1974 and 1975, the per capita amount devoted to pensions, education, and the like rose by 12 per cent in real terms, with a large share of the gain due to the introduction of a program of food subsidies.[27] New claims for unemployment benefits placed an additional demand upon the Treasury, which sought to cut back where it could. The Treasury could exercise little control, for the fastest-growing programs were those of local governments; the personal social services, for example, increased by 13.8 per cent, a rate only slightly below that of the preceding years.[28] Since the economy generated little new revenue, higher rates of taxation and double-digit inflation were inevitable, and they devoured disposable income. Like the sorcerer's broom in the fairy tale, the British welfare state, a manageable instrument in normal times, has proved to be a demonic one in the strained conditions the nation now confronts.

REDISTRIBUTION AND WELFARE

Measuring a welfare state's claim on its country's *total* resources is one way of assessing its impact. Another, certainly more direct, is by examining its effect on *individual* resources. At least in theory, a nation like Britain, which devotes more than half of its national product to the public sector, could apportion the cost evenly among its population. Alternately, it could tax its wealthier citizens more heavily to provide benefits for its poorer ones. If done this way, a seemingly affordable share of total resources would hide a much greater demand upon the income and wealth of the most productive individuals. Through such redistribution, an expanding welfare state might effectively undercut national growth.

This is the converse of the pampering theory. A generous social policy is harmful not because it encourages a life of state-supported indolence, but because it discourages the efforts of those most likely to succeed. *Some* redistribution must occur in a welfare state; even if everyone pays the same amount, not everyone has the same need for the services and benefits provided. If there is a progressive tax as well, there will be additional penalties placed on individual enterprise. And if the standards of public provision become inordinately high, so too will the financial disincentives. Effort may decline, tax evasion commence, residence in Switzerland or elsewhere be considered. Is this what has occurred in Britain?

Again a simple answer will not suffice. Since the creation of the welfare state, there has been a modest change in the distribution of income and wealth toward greater equality.

But it has proceeded no more rapidly in the entire period than in the six years of war prior to it. Moreover, the primary redistributive means of taxation and transfer payments have generally been less important than the creation of new forms of wealth or than shifts in the sources of income. Although the data in this area are complex, they do not reveal the welfare state as the engine of equality that its advocates desired and its critics decried.

If there is an exception to this conclusion, it is for the very rich. The pretax incomes of the top 1 per cent of British households have been cut in half since 1949, falling from an 11.2 per cent share of total income to 6.4 per cent in 1973. Largely as a result, the shares of the top 5 and 10 per cent have also declined.[29] But the trend was less severe *after* income taxes. The top 1 per cent had 6.4 per cent of all income after paying the Inland Revenue in 1949 and 4.4 per cent after doing so in 1973.[30] In the interim, the welfare state had expanded enormously, but the bill to the wealthiest was relatively lighter.

For the remaining households, the gains have varied. The lower half has obtained little since the war. It had 23.7 per cent of the pretax income in 1949 and 24 per cent in 1973; after income taxes, its share increased by the same amount.[31] The middle and upper-middle classes, however, improved their positions. From 43.1 per cent in 1949, their income rose to 49.1 per cent of the total by 1973, with most of the gain occurring before 1959. But *after* taxes, their resources grew less quickly: from 46.4 per cent to 49.7 per cent during the postwar period.[32] As the welfare state became larger, the middle classes prospered, though they also paid relatively more for its services.

Adding the effects of other taxes, transfer payments, and in-kind benefits such as education gives a different picture. The overall impact of British social policy seems more markedly redistributive. In the period between 1961 and

1963, the Gini coefficient—a measure that is 0 at complete equality and 100 at complete inequality—was 40.3 for pre-tax income, but 32.8 after all taxes and benefits were included. Ten years later, the figures were 42.3 and 32.4, respectively.[33] However, these figures exaggerate the amount of change. Nearly one quarter of the apparent shift came from assuming that the full cost of health care, schooling, and the like is the real value of these services to the recipients, a procedure apt to overstate their worth. Moreover, most of the redistribution occurred at the extremes of the income scale. In the 1961–63 period, the share of the top 10 per cent declined by 3.9 points after all taxes and benefits were figured, while that of the bottom 30 per cent rose by the same amount. Then, and to a lesser degree a decade afterward, the middle classes neither gained nor lost from the transactions.

Social policy has had less to do with this gradual movement toward equality than have two significant changes in British society. The country now has more employees and managers and relatively fewer rentiers. Since 1938, and even 1949, a greater share of personal income has come from wages, salaries, and the like, and a smaller one from rents, dividends, and interest, the primary sources of money for the rich.[34] In addition, the size of the elderly population has increased. Since many have few resources of their own, they subsist to a large extent on social benefits. Hence, even a modest standard of provision is bound to bring greater equality of incomes. Indeed, simple growth in the number of pensioners accounts for the larger decline in the Gini coefficient in 1971–73 than a decade earlier.

While these social characteristics have nudged the country toward equality, another has limited the possible scope of policy: By international standards, the pretax distribution of British income is already fairly egalitarian. Some calculations by A. B. Atkinson, for instance, show a Gini coefficient of 38 for the United States in 1967 and 30 for Britain the following year.[35] To be among the top 10 per cent in 1973, a "tax unit" (usually a household) needed earnings of £2,857, or a bit more than $7,000.[36] Over half of all American families obtained as much. Where the range of incomes is so narrow, the potential for extensive redistribution is necessarily slight. Thus the impact of taxation alone has been nearly proportional. In 1972, indirect levies, such as sales taxes, broadened the range of incomes by only slightly less than direct levies reduced it.[37] To the extent that the welfare state has promoted equality, it has done so by leveling up, rather than down.

It is in the distribution of personal wealth that the greatest changes have occurred. Just before the war, the top 1 per cent of the adult population held 56 per cent of all wealth, and the bottom 90 per cent held a mere 12 per cent.[38] By 1960, the share of the topmost had fallen to 42 per cent, and then to 27.6 per cent in 1973.[39] Meanwhile, the bottom 90 per cent had come to own fully one third of the nation's wealth.[40]

The shift was not the result of any socialist program to confiscate the holdings of the aristocracy. Britain still has no tax on wealth—a Labour-led Parliamentary committee recently could not agree to recommend one—and its inheritance duties seem designed chiefly to tax the ingenuity of estate lawyers. Rather, major changes in the composition of personal wealth have taken place. In 1960, physical assets, primarily houses, amounted to 30.4 per cent of all holdings; in 1973, they were nearly half. The value of financial assets, such as stocks and securities, declined by the same extent.[41] The distribution of wealth became more equal as an increasing number of Britons used their earnings to purchase homes, refrigerators, cars, and similar goods. Indeed, if pension rights were included, the amount of redistribution would be even more impressive. According to the Royal Commission on the Distribution of Income and Wealth, the share of the top 1 per cent would drop by one third and the share of the bottom 80 per cent would more than double.[42] Although personal wealth is still not as evenly divided as income, the welfare state seemingly offers no great barrier to its accumulation, at least for those likely to be skilled workers, managers, and professionals.

At any particular moment, to be sure, the incidence of taxes and benefits of British social policy is sharply progressive. As social spending has grown, the upper- and, increasingly, the middle-income Briton has found himself losing more through taxes—perhaps, much more—than he gained from welfare-state benefits. A young professional couple, for example, with above-average salaries and little need for the health services, schools, or pensions, may find its income substantially reduced. Yet this has had little cumulative effect on the British income distribution, largely because, over a normal lifetime, the balance improves as these various social programs are used. Redistribution takes place not only from richer to poorer, but also from the healthy to the ill, from single adults to families, from younger to older, and in numerous other ways. This complicated system might well discourage the industrious. At the same time it might just as easily encourage harder work by those who prefer to earn and spend for the day, and to lay aside few of their own resources for the uncertainties of the future; their security now guaranteed by their taxes, such people might now work harder so as to increase their discretionary post-tax income.

THE SERVICES STATE

The irony is that as the welfare state has made Britons more secure, it has made their nation less so.

There is nothing mysterious in this. Britain may indeed have spent no more on social programs than comparable countries have. It may have been moderate in committing its resources to these activities. It may even have managed to provide adequate incentives to earn and to save. Yet it has done all this while its industries have been contracting. The result is that the welfare state has been the growth sector of the British economy, especially in recent years. Britons have increasingly become employed in "doing good." And that has meant that the nation was almost certainly less likely to do well.

In all countries, the pattern is similar. As they become wealthier and more highly developed, jobs in agriculture and manufacturing decline, while those providing services —insurance, banking, law, health care, education, and the like—increase. Only indirectly, if at all, will the latter add to national income. An educated worker presumably can produce more valuable goods than an uneducated one. But in the process of schooling, resources are diverted that might be worth more than the return due to increased skills. If a nation is to remain prosperous, its industries must make good at least some of the loss. In most of Europe and in the United States, that is what has occurred. In Britain, it has not.

In most Common Market countries, the growth of the services sector has been offset by a decline in agricultural employment, but in Britain, the decline has instead been in manufacturing. Thus, from 1960 to 1973, while the services sector was expanding from 47 per cent to 54.7 per cent of the labor force, the percentage of British workers employed in agriculture dropped from 4 per cent to 3 per cent, and that in industry from 49 per cent to 42.3 per cent. In France, during the same period, industry's share of the labor force remained constant at 39 per cent, even as the share of services rose from 38.6 per cent to 48.4 per cent. Likewise, about 48 per cent of West German workers were engaged in manufacturing or related areas in 1960 and again in 1973; meanwhile, services had grown from 37.8 per cent to 43.6 per cent. Only in Belgium, the Netherlands, and Denmark did the proportion of industrial jobs decline at all, and in these, the rate was approximately half that in Britain.[43]

One has to look to Sweden or the United States to find a performance similar to Britain's. In both, the growth of the services sector has been accompanied by a sharp decline in the proportion of the work force in manufacturing. But there is also an important difference. During the 1960s and early 1970s, industrial employment in the two countries increased absolutely while it decreased proportionally. In Britain, the decline was absolute as well as relative. By 1971, the textile industry employed 200,000 fewer workers than it had a decade earlier; shipbuilding, 66,000 fewer; leather, clothing, and footwear, 88,000 fewer; automobiles and other vehicles, 27,000 fewer. If these trends continued, the Department of Employment predicted that another 500,000 jobs in manufacturing would disappear in the 1970s, while the rest of the economy would add more than 1 million.[44] The nation's current condition suggests this may be an overly optimistic forecast.

Not all of this loss in output went unreplaced. Some industries became more efficient, and some services made real contributions to the economy. In banking and insurance, for example, Britain added nearly 250,000 workers during the 1960s.[45] For a nation chronically in need of capital, this would not appear to be an unwise use of its resources. Indeed, London's financial community is a major asset, despite the diminished role of sterling in international commerce.

But these types of services did not grow as rapidly as education, health care, social services, and public administration. From 1961 to 1973, the work force in central government increased by 14 per cent, and in local government, by 53 per cent.[46] By 1981, the Employment Department's survey projected, a total of 2 million new jobs will have been created in the public sector.[47]

These probably added something to national income, but it is not easy to say how much. For one, the expansion of the public services brought more women and part-time workers into the labor force. But if they could have been employed in industry, their contributions might well have been more valuable.[48] Public spending also stimulated demand for certain goods, both directly through the purchase of textbooks, medicines, and the like, and indirectly, as a result of steady (and higher) pay for teachers, doctors, and providers of other services. This presumably had some value in sustaining the British economy, but whether investment elsewhere would have been still more productive is another matter. Indeed, given the low return to spending in education, health care, and similar programs, it is hard to imagine that a different pattern of growth would not have done better.[49] Even if these services had enhanced the health, education, or well-being of Britons, the payoff could not have been great. Healthier and better-educated workers, no less than their opposites, confronted a shortage of opportunities in the industrial sector. Whatever its personal value, the welfare state could not yield much in the way of economic rewards (except, of course, to those countries fortunate to receive British emigrants), for the jobs that were most likely to be available were those that could, perhaps, increase "human" capital, but little else.

Thus the British predicament. As in Sweden and the United States, providing services is now the occupation of a majority of the labor force, including the one out of six who work in the public sector. Britain differs from Sweden and the United States (and even more from other countries still moving in the same direction) in that industrial growth has been laggard. More Britons are employed in tasks that add little or nothing to national output; fewer have jobs that could generate greater income, and even these usually do not do very well. In essence, Britain has evolved into a poor man's version of the postindustrial state.

How this came about is a complex tale. It involves changes in the competitive position of British firms, in the availability of capital, and in governmental industrial policies. And, of course, it also involves productivity. According to the National Economic Development Office, Britain obtains a smaller increase in output from each unit of capital invested than any other industrialized country.[50] Numerous reasons might be suggested to explain this phenomenon: obsolete plant and machinery, formal and informal work rules, misdirected investments, and so on. I have made no effort to determine which (if any) are most important.

What I have done is argue that the programs of the welfare state deserve relatively little of the blame. Based on the indirect evidence presented here, they do not appear to have pampered the British worker nor to have drastically cut his financial incentives. (At least not so far; the rapid increase in social spending of the past few years may be changing the situation.) Moreover, such damage as might have occurred could well have been offset by improvements in the quality of the labor force. Though unlikely to have hampered the performance of industry, nonetheless, the welfare state has diverted the careers of many Britons away from it, and in this way it has helped make an already weak economy even weaker. For Britain is now a specialist in producing welfare, a commodity that will do little to improve the balance of trade or the myriad of problems with which the nation is beset.

Was—is—there an alternative? On the premise that there is, the Labour government's latest industrial policy is founded. It would restrain the growth of social programs while encouraging the expansion of productive industries. The Conservatives, should they return to office, would pursue a similar course, though perhaps with more fervor.[51] Neither is likely to have much success.

This is partly due to the difficulties in assisting, let alone identifying, potentially viable firms. Success depends upon the ability to foresee changes in demand, in the price of raw materials, and in the products of competitors. For Britain, the problems are compounded by the country's dependence upon international trade. Past industrial policies provide few grounds for optimism.[52]

In any event, government actions can rarely be based on economic criteria alone. Preserving jobs, regional prosperity, or a symbolic presence in an industry (such as automobiles) will also be considered, in addition to any political calculations. Thus, despite its own internal reports, the Labour government helped "bail out" the Chrysler Corporration, just as the previous Conservative government aided such "lame ducks" (to use the term of the Cabinet minister responsible) as Rolls-Royce. Perhaps inevitably, industrial policies will be more protective than ruthless, creating a quasi-nationalized enterprise out of one otherwise apt to founder. To achieve growth in manufacturing, there is no real substitute for making sound fiscal and monetary decisions.

That, too, is difficult, since British governments have consistently overestimated their abilities to reduce public spending. This is not because it is uncontrollable, in the sense that the amount expended on pensions is determined mainly by the number who claim them. Even then, benefit levels can be adjusted to lower costs or eligibility, as by revising them annually instead of semiannually. Moreover, since their major outlays are for facilities and staff, most other programs can be budgeted. Rather, the problem is that even in the midst of an economic crisis, no British government will be able (or think itself able) to muster support for budget cuts.

The welfare state expanded because most Britons wanted what it provides. It resists contraction because they want still more. Britons want public jobs that are better paying than equivalent ones in the private sector. They want subsidies; the February 1974 elections, which returned Harold Wilson to office, resulted in a prompt £10 hike in aid to the elderly, who gratefully increased their support for him the following October. Most importantly, Britons want services that are generally deemed proper and useful. In one of those rare instances where political language reveals almost as much as it conceals, the term "social wage" has lately come to stand for the per capita amount of welfare spending. Presumably, out of take-home pay one buys a car, a home, and holidays abroad; out of the "social wage" one purchases health care, education, and a decent retirement. The latter, as the Institute of Economic Affairs (IEA) has proposed, might be more efficiently bought out-of-pocket, but would it matter? Given an additional £1,500, a 1970 IEA survey showed, a sample of Britons would have used more than half to obtain "welfare" goods.[53] At the time (and still today), the proportion of national income actually being spent on social programs was much smaller.

So long as such demand persists, it is hardly surprising that the real issue is not how to limit the welfare state, but how to finance it. Except for the occasional imposition of user charges, there has been little interest in letting consumers pay directly. (Even then, payment of a small fee for prescriptions or school milk is unlikely to have much impact upon demand.) Instead, British governments have tried, with decreasing success, to expand the nation's capacity for social spending. For Conservatives, this has meant advocating cuts in taxation; for Labour, a range of measures, including applied technology, devaluation, a "social contract," and most recently, a tax reduction linked to a ceiling on wage increases. While curbing the welfare state was often threatened, it was rarely accomplished. Just as the Heath government's efforts yielded almost invisible results, so too would the much-heralded "austerity" plan of the Wilson-Callaghan administration. Indeed, most of the proposed reductions amount to postponing projects still on the drawing board or not filling positions in the civil service as they become vacant. In case even these measures prove too restrictive, the Labour government is committed to modify them "'as the general course of the economy and the most important needs of the community require.' "54 Until more factory hands are seen to be at least as necessary as extra playleaders, group workers, and program coordinators, no real trimming of the welfare state will occur.

One doubts that this will happen soon. Understandably, hard times make retrenchment difficult; the memory of the inadequacy of social services during the Depression is still strong. In addition, no substantial political force appears ready to take on the task. The social reforms of Disraeli give British Conservatives as good a claim to the patrimony of the welfare state as Labour has; indeed, the postwar history has largely been one of socialists expanding programs while in office, and Tories preserving or improving them. (Lest it be thought that change is in the offing, it is worth recalling that one of Margaret Thatcher's major acts as Minister of Education was to call for a massive increase in public nursery school enrollment.) With a firm hand in the Treasury, North Sea oil, and good luck, Britain's economy may pick up again, thereby making social spending nearly as manageable as it was a decade ago. If the services themselves become more productive, further improvement might follow. But the basic problem is one of choice. Precisely because the British attached great value to welfare programs, the nation has been a world leader in social policy. Because it continues to do so, Britain will remain less prosperous as well.

Englanditis

Peter Jay

We in Britain are a confused and unhappy people. So are those of our fellows on the Continent of Western Europe who have their wits about them. So too are our many friends in the United States who rightly see in the anguish of the United Kingdom the advanced stages of a disease that has already taken hold throughout Western Europe and that is beginning to show its unmistakable symptoms in the United States.

There may or may not be anything we can do about the grounds for our unhappiness, which as things stand is thoroughly well founded. But there is no need to be confused. We can try at least to understand the basis of our morbidity, even if this requires some acutely painful reassessments of cherished institutions and values.

We are unhappy because the foundations of our prosperity seem to be eroding faster and faster and because we can neither find nor agree upon any sure remedy for this decay. We are confused because we do not clearly understand why all this is happening to us, whether it is due to the malefactions of subversive groups, the incompetence of governments, defects of national character, the rhythms of history, the luck of the draw, or what.

The search for someone to blame adds to the confusion and the bitterness. Government and governed become more and more alienated from one another. The governors believe the governed to be irretrievably greedy, feckless, idle, and recalcitrant, while the governed believe the governors to be stupid, corrupt, power-crazed, and unrepresentative. Likewise class is set against class, the middle classes denouncing the rapacity of the workers, while the workers rail at the privileges and the hypocrisy of the better off.

In Britain region is set against region, and separatism gains steady support in Ulster, in Scotland, in Wales, and, by reaction, in England itself. Only the Labour Party can any longer claim a vestige of nationwide support, and even it could not get even 30 per cent of the potential electorate to support it in 1974; but for London and Bristol, the Labour Party would be virtually unrepresented from the whole of the south of England.

The fissures spread out in all directions like an ice fall: disintegration in slow motion. Labor unions, business management, and city financiers are locked in a triangle of mutual vituperation and incomprehension. Union leaders point to the lack of investment in productive industry. Industrialists complain that the capital markets and the banks do not support them because the financiers' time horizons are too short and their understanding of industry is negligible. And the investors ask how they can be expected to put up capital when the unions pre-empt all, or more than all, the potential return on new plant and equipment.

Weak labor unions with low-paid members loudly support same-all-'round ceilings on pay increases while their stronger brothers, in entrenched industrial positions with higher-paid workers, stoutly defend their "differentials" and angrily compare their lot with the standards enjoyed by bloated capitalists, whom they still imagine—not always wrongly—to be living like a caricature of a nineteenth-century railway baron. The media criticize everyone and everything; and almost everyone blames the media for the lack of national unanimity and commitment.

It is an unedifying spectacle and an unprofitable arrangement. Nor does it touch at any point on the true causes of the problem. These causes are deep-seated and general, embedded in the very organization of our society. They are also complex and abstract. Therefore they are little perceived; and the analysis of them cannot compete with the more readily intelligible, concrete, and enjoyable sport of exposing "guilty men" and baiting those who are in what is supposed to be "power." There are no guilty men, of course, but there are defective institutions.

The political and economic organization of modern liberal democracies is dedicated, above all, to the satisfaction of individual wants. How are we to establish what individuals want? By asking them. How are we to ensure that they get what they want, at least so far as possible? By letting them make the decisions. How do we arrange that? By letting them elect their governments and by letting them spend their money in a free competitive marketplace.

This engagingly simple political philosophy may indeed have been a useful antidote to the depredations practiced on mankind by authoritarian and paternalist regimes in the name of higher values. But, alas, it already has built into it the tension—historicists might say the contradiction—that lies at the root of our present troubles. For, as the great Austrian economist Joseph Schumpeter pointed out, the marketplace for votes and the marketplace for goods operate according to vastly different and frequently incompatible criteria. When the domains of the economic and political marketplaces overlap—as they often do—they come into serious conflict.

The political arena is a marketplace in votes. Rival teams organize themselves to win a majority or at least a plurality of support so that they can exercise power. The only cost of voting for one team is that you cannot vote for another. The teams naturally and inevitably seek to outbid each other by offering more of whatever they think the voters want. There is no mechanism that requires the bids to be internally consistent or forces voters to balance more of one good against more of another.

The economic arena is—or at least supposedly starts out as—a marketplace in money. But here the individual chooses quite differently. He makes small decisions all the time instead of one big decision every few years. Each decision is marginal, to spend his next penny on a little more of this rather than a little more of that. He does not have to pledge all of his income for the next few years to one of a short list of comprehensive packages.

Thus, the economic and political marketplaces offer different incentives to entrepreneurs. The political entrepreneur asks what most people want. The economic entrepreneur must ask himself what people want most. Intensity of wants becomes all-important where the person choosing has to give up something—namely, the opportunity to spend money on something else—each time he chooses.

Second, in the economic case the coin in which the chooser casts his vote—the money he pays for his purchases—is also the resource that the supplier needs to continue and maybe expand the process of supply. In the political case, while votes are the bases of power, they are not the material that power uses. The command over the resources of power comes from the taxing power, which is awarded by a plurality of votes. There is no mechanism for ensuring that a plurality of votes implies a commitment by the voters of the quantum of resources needed to fulfill the program on which the winning political team has won an election.

The economic marketplace requires the citizen to exercise his choice and to commit the resources needed to fulfill it in the single act of purchase whereby he parts with his money. This essential feature of the price mechanism, together with the assumption that individuals will normally seek their own best economic advantage as both consumers and suppliers, is the foundation of liberal economics.

It is the "invisible hand" that economists since Adam Smith have recognized as the built-in guarantee not only of consistency in economic choices, but also of the optimal matching of available resources to individual wants. Of course, everyone is familiar with a thousand and one different ways in which the process does not operate or is prevented from operating in this idealized fashion. Perhaps the most widely quoted of these defects is that purchasing power, post-tax as well as pretax, is unequal and must necessarily be so, if the market is to have incentives for serving individual wants.

These imperfections have provided the political pretext, though not the main motive, for intervention by government in the economic domain. It is not necessary here to review the vast literature on the proper scope for the limits of such intervention. Suffice it to say that there is nothing in the operation of the political marketplace that requires that those limits be observed.

Indeed, the essence of democratic politics is a gigantic celebration of the fact that you *can* get something for nothing, or at least that *you*—the individual voter—can get something for nothing, even if as the ancients had it, *ex nihilo nihil fit*; for government, with its legalized powers of coercion, can award benefits here while it charges costs there. That indeed is the whole nature of the redistribution of wealth and income, an almost universally accepted function of government.

The point here is not to question the legitimacy of this aspect of the political process, but to emphasize that it is a process without any sensitive or automatic regulator. In the very long run, it may be argued, societies will discover that it does not pay them to sacrifice too much of the incentive functions of incomes to the cause of equality or "fairness"; but any such feedback is problematic and highly uncertain.

The conflict between the different logics of political and economic choice is most clearly manifest in the relationship between unemployment and inflation. Since Keynes, since the war, since the British *Employment Policy* White Paper of 1944, and since the American Employment Act of 1946, a pledge of full employment has been an indispensable ingredient in any bid for electoral victory.

After the experiences of the 1930s, almost every voter— or so all politicians have assumed—has regarded the avoidance of mass unemployment as an overriding political objective. After the writings of Keynes and even more after the simplified popularization of his writings and their endorsement by government, the politicians and the public have also assumed that the means of securing high employment always lay at hand.

Whenever unemployment looked like it was rising to politically embarrassing levels—and the threshold of embarrassment was extremely low by previous historical standards—the response was to put more spending power into people's pockets, whether by cutting taxes, increasing government spending, or easing credit conditions through monetary policy.

It was recognized in theory that one might go too far in this direction, overheat the economy, and cause inflation. But it was not doubted that there was a safe zone in which something approaching full employment could be maintained without running risks of serious inflation. The exact tradeoffs within that zone between degrees of full employment and degrees of price stability were thought to be described by a stable relationship know as the "Phillips curve."

The economic realities were unhappily different. The belief that, outside the narrow range of the Phillips curve, the regulation of spending power (known as "demand management") affected the price level alone or the employment level alone, according to whether the pressure of demand was above or below the full employment zone, was false.

The truth is that in the short term—for the first year or two—demand management mainly affects the real volume of spending, output, and therefore employment, while in the longer run it mainly affects the price level. The notion inherent in the popular understanding of Keynes—that an economy could be indefinitely underemployed through deficient demand without prices eventually being forced down sufficiently to clear markets, including the labor market—was a dangerous misunderstanding of the unhappy experiences of the 1930s.

Nonetheless, the belief was almost universal in British economic circles and increasingly predominant in American and Continental European circles that, provided actual overheating of the economy was avoided (and with it "overfull employment"), budget deficits and the associated expansion of the money supply could be used more or less without limit to head off any incipient rise in unemployment.

At the same time, there were objective reasons why unemployment was likely to rise above the levels regarded as "full employment," even in the absence of any positively deflationary actions by government and the central bank. These were and are of two kinds, both barely recognized and little understood: the general imperfections of the labor market; and the operation of what is variously known as "free collective bargaining" and as "trade union monopoly bargaining."

Imperfections of the labor market include anything that keeps job seekers and vacancies from being instantly matched to one another. As the pattern of demand and the techniques of supply constantly evolve, different kinds of workers are required by different entrepreneurs in different places. It takes time to convert some workers from one role to another. Others can never be converted and have to be replaced by a new and differently trained generation.

There is a real personal cost to moving, which often makes workers willing to remain unemployed, sometimes indefinitely, rather than take work in a faraway place. People are naturally reluctant to pull up the roots of family, friendship, and all the familiarities of "home," and they are further discouraged by British public housing regulations which automatically take away an occupier's title to very low-rent accommodation if he moves to another district.

And there are a thousand and one other major and minor frictions that normally result in a degree of mismatch, at any moment in time, between labor force and work opportunities. The mismatch cannot but be reflected in a margin of the work force being out of work, or at least between jobs, at any one time. The size of that margin, of course, will also depend on the capital endowment of industry and on its rate of change in relation to the rate of change of the skills of the work force.

This margin may, in Professor Milton Friedman's words, be called the "natural" rate of unemployment, although this should not be taken to mean that it is established by any law of nature. It is just a catch-all phrase for all the circumstances *other than the manipulation of monetary demand by governments* that influence the level of unemployment.

The role of free collective bargaining may be regarded as a second and separate reason why conventional postwar full employment policies were incompatible with price stability—or indeed with a stable rate of inflation—or it can be seen as a special case of the first general reason. The latter way of putting it emphasizes the monopolistic character of collective bargaining by labor unions. The effect of charging a monopoly price for labor must inevitably be to reduce "sales," that is, employment, below the market-clearing level. Some people will get paid more than they would under perfect competition in the labor market, but others will not get jobs at all.

The effect, therefore, of a widespread pattern of monopolistic bargaining in the labor market will be to increase the numbers unemployed—in other words, to raise the "natural" rate of unemployment. This, as has often been pointed out, is in itself a once-and-for-all effect. But like the once-and-for-all effects of other labor market imperfections, it gives rise to an accelerating, eventually explosive rate of inflation when it is combined with a government commitment to maintain by demand management a lower rate of unemployment than this new "natural level."

As soon as the level of unemployment begins to approach the higher "natural" rate, government rushes in with injections of additional spending power, whether by fiscal or monetary means. These monetary or fiscal injections initially increase demand and so check or reverse the rise in unemployment. But this creates an imbalance of supply and demand in the labor market. Either unemployment is now below the natural rate, or it is below the rate that is needed just to inhibit the further exercise of labor unions' monopoly bargaining power.

In consequence, the price of labor rises once again. If final prices are not raised to cover this, businesses close and unemployment rises once again. If prices do go up, consumers' incomes will buy less, the volume of sales falls, output falls, and unemployment rises once again. Whereupon government is forced to intervene again with another injection of extra spending power. Before long, consumers and pay bargainers—indeed, everyone involved in the economy—gets used to continuing inflation. It becomes built into expectations, and so the stimulative effects of any given amount of governmental "reflation" are eroded. Governments then begin to increase the dose; and there is no end to this process of trying to keep the actual inflation rate permanently ahead of constantly catching-up expectations until the stage of hyperinflation—and breadown—is reached.

It is not strictly necessary, however, to express the role of free collective bargaining by labor unions as a special case of the natural-rate-of-unemployment hypothesis. More simply, it can be said that in anything short of a total buyers' market for labor—which would imply a level of unemployment many times greater than any postwar government has even contemplated—labor monopolies can progressively force up the price of labor.

Since there is no corresponding increase in the value of output, the extra claims on the available resources have to be neutralized by rising prices, which then become the bases for the next round of pay claims. It may well be that the sum of all the monopoly pay claims, expressed in terms of the real purchasing power demanded, is greater than the national output available to satisfy them. In that case, equilibrium in the short term can only be maintained if inflation continuously runs ahead of the inflationary expectations of the pay bargainers or if the labor monopolies are permitted to price themselves out of their jobs until they are deterred from further exercise of their market power. Since governments are pledged not to let the second happen, they are forced to choose the other horn of the dilemma and to inflate at an accelerating rate.

Surely, it will be said, Western democracy is not going to wreck itself on such absurd and obvious nonsense. Unfortunately, it probably will, at least on the eastern side of the Atlantic. The problem is only beginning to be recognized very late in the day because it operates transcyclically rather than intracyclically.

Public attention has been and largely remains focused on the intracyclical ebbs and flows of output, employment, and inflation (see Table). This has enabled lay people and even some economists constantly to deceive themselves that

The cyclical fickleness of public opinion in Britain is shown
in the results of a poll taken over recent years by the
Opinion Research Centre, a British polling organization:

TREND IN RELATIVE IMPORTANCE OF INFLATION AND UNEMPLOYMENT

Q. What do you yourself feel are the most important problems the
government should do something about? Anything else?

	Prices/rising prices/ cost of living	Unemployment situation/ unemployment too high	*Memo* Increase in retail prices over previous 12 months	Unemployment (Gt. Britain seasonally adjusted)
	%	%	%	%
Jan.'72	34	61	8.9	3.8
Jul.'73	55	6	9.4	2.5
Oct.'73	52	6	9.2	2.2
Feb.'74	58	5	13.2	2.4
Mar.'74	64	6	13.5	2.4
Jun.'74	43	3	16.5	2.5
Aug.'74	53	8	16.9	2.6
Oct.'74	64	8	17.0	2.7
Feb.'75	56	13	19.9	3.1
May '75	59	19	25.0	3.6
Sept.'75	57	32	26.6	4.4
Oct.'75	53	36	25.9	4.6
Jan.'76	49	48	23.4	5.1

*NOTE: References to food prices were not coded separately in the first
survey and the last two.

The shifts in public priorities follow closely the movements of the economic cycle.

the prevailing economic evil of the moment—inflation, unemployment, or balance-of-payments deficit—was always about to be cured. They have not noticed that from cycle to cycle the relationship among these alternative expressions of the unattainability of "full employment" has been deteriorating.

It takes more and more inflation (or bigger and bigger balance-of-payments deficits, which are in some circumstances an inflation substitute) to achieve—or, more often, to fail to achieve—any given employment level. This evidence has been overlooked because we have all been watching the ends of the seesaw go up and down, without seeing that the fulcrum on which the whole contraption rests is steadily rising.

Even if the danger is fully appreciated, it is far from clear that the right action will be possible. The logic of ballot-box choice enables us—indeed, almost forces us—to vote for full employment without thereby also voting for the means to achieve it, which must include a willingness to sell one's own labor at a market-clearing price. Even that would not be enough. Everyone else would have to be committed to such individual bargaining; and that would imply the end of collective bargaining and therefore of labor unions in their main historic role.

It would further be necessary to vote for other measures that would reduce the "natural" level of unemployment until it coincided with our chosen definition of full employment. This could certainly include in Britain an end to subsidized municipal housing (total transferability of the right to cheap homes enjoyed by public housing occupants being in practice impossible).

Thus, even though the mass of voters may very well dislike inflation more than they dislike unemployment, the logic of ballot-box choice may still give rise to inflationary policies. For voters can vote against inflation—or imagine they are voting against inflation—but to actually stop inflation they would have to vote against collective bargaining, housing subsidies, and the like. Even the statesman who fully perceives the nature of the dilemma is debarred from campaigning accordingly. He knows—or thinks he knows—that this would be the road to political extinction, which, as he will say, solves nothing.

Likewise, the fully intelligent citizen is debarred from voting for an option that no party puts forward. Even if the fully perceptive statesman and the fully intelligent voter could somehow establish contact, it is still not certain that it would be rational for the voter to support the statesman. The voter may fear the certainty of a deep and prolonged recession for three or four years more than he fears the eventual crash to which he knows traditional policies must one day lead.

At this point it will be objected that the mechanisms of political and economic choice are being made the scapegoats for the much simpler vice of wrong choices, most conspicuously for wrong choices by the British electorate. This would only be true if it were supposed that voters had no other objectives at all but, for example, stable prices, or that whenever they will an end, they also will the means.

But the whole point made here is that voters, like other men, have multiple objectives and that the logic of political choice dissociates means from end. It can well be argued that, if an able political candidate or party explained "the facts" to the voters and convinced them of the connections among inflation, collective bargaining, and unemployment, the voters might decide to modify the priority they implicitly gave to one of these objectives.

But how? Political choices are not presented like social survey questionnaires, as a matter of arranging objectives on an ordinal scale in sequence of preference, with weights attached. They are presented as choices among named individuals.

True, one could vote for the individual who presented the most realistic tradeoffs combined with one's preferred sequence of preference. But will not that candidate always be outbid by the candidate who offers more of all the objectives, without regard to any realistic tradeoffs among them?

Conceivably not, if the voters are wise, well-informed, and prone to skepticism about politicians. But it also requires that other politicians should expect the voters to be so minded. Otherwise the virtuous political platform will be chased out of the campaign by the panglossian candidate; and not even the wise, well-informed, and skeptical voter will be able to vote for it.

It will be said again that a candidate could offer the electorate a pledge to end collective bargaining and that he could win, so far as the ballot box mechanism is concerned. So he could. But why should people vote for him? They do not—normally—disapprove of collective bargaining as a thing in itself, as they disapprove of rising prices, unemployment, pollution, taxes, and other immediate aggravations.

The candidate would have to argue that it should be ended as a means to other ends, namely, stopping inflation or permitting full employment to be restored consistently with stable prices. Immediately his argument can be attacked.

Other candidates will say it is not so. Of course, inflation must be stopped. Full employment must be maintained. But vote for me and you can have all of that and collective bargaining too. Why vote for the man who offers less?

The only possible reason to vote for him is because you believe he might actually deliver. But that is once again to suppose that voters and political candidates will connect means and ends and that each will believe that the other will so connect means and ends. There is nothing but bitter experience to make this a characteristic of ballot-box choice, especially when the links between means and ends are as controversial as in economics.

The problem then is that the logic of ballot-box choice does not coincide with, and almost certainly contradicts, the logic of economic optimization. Government is bound to get drawn into roles and programs that are bound to reduce economic welfare below the otherwise attainable optimum. The full employment-inflation dilemma is only the most important of these because it produces an explosive chain reaction that is destructive not merely of a finite quantum of welfare but also of the whole system.

Nor is this dilemma in any way solved by political programs that would seek to command economic variables to behave contrary to their own nature. Incomes policies, however rational and enlightened they may appear when looked at from the macro level, necessarily become arbitrary and unacceptable when seen at the micro level, as they are by all the individuals on whose consent such programs, except in totalitarian states, totally depend. Such arbitrariness is occasionally tolerated for a few months in a fit of national fervor, but it never has and never could last longer.

So we reach the depressing conclusion that the operation of free democracy appears to force governments into positions (the commitment to full employment) that prevent them from taking steps (fiscal and monetary restraint) that are necessary to arrest the menace (accelerating inflation) that threatens to undermine the condition (stable prosperity) on which political stability and therefore liberal democracy depend. In other words, democracy has itself by the tail and is eating itself up fast.

There is nothing inevitable, in the absolute sense, about a process that consists entirely of human actions. We could all decide to travel a different route; but that is an extremely difficult thing for people in groups of many millions to do in the absence of a system that reconciles public with private goods and that harmonizes the logic of political choice with the logic of economic choice.

If any nation is likely to escape the dilemma, it is the United States, because it combines a comparatively mild form of the complaint with far and away the toughest political institutions of any Western country. Inflation is more unpopular in the United States than in almost any other industrial country, except perhaps West Germany. The American labor market is markedly less unionized; and there is a very large sector of genuinely individual pay bargaining in the United States.

This means that it is more likely that an American government can and will find political support for a strong stand against inflation, even at the price of several years of high unemployment by postwar standards. It also means that political authority will be better able to withstand any given amount of direct revolutionary challenge that a period of economic adversity produces. Finally, many Americans still harbor a strong ideological commitment to political and economic liberties, and will defend them beyond any short-term calculation of standard of living.

These advantages may well mean that, as the dilemma worsens toward the critical choice between a long recession and the final plunge into hyperinflation, the United States will manage to draw back. By the mid- or late 1980s, price stability in the United States may be reconciled with recovering prosperity; and at the same time, congressmen may still be elected every two years, Presidents every four, and senators every six in accordance with an unchanged Constitution.

It is hard to be so sanguine about Western Europe, where the economic weakness is greater and where political institutions have shallower foundations. Countries like Britain, which do have a long tradition of political continuity, face the economic dilemma in its most highly developed form.

Countries like West Germany, which face less acute economic dilemmas, have the weakest political institutions and are therefore vulnerable to even a mild degree of economic adversity. Others, like Italy, have the worst of both worlds. In consequence, they have already slipped over the abyss and must soon be dashed on the waiting rocks of political anarchy and economic deprivation.

It can be objected that the experience of the United States, West Germany, and other countries practicing ballot-box democracy disproves, rather than confirms, the thesis that the contradiction between the imperatives of the political marketplace and the imperatives of economic stability is creating an unstable and potentially disastrous reliance on accelerating inflation. Just because different countries have advanced different distances along this road, and because these differences appear to be traceable, at least in part, to differing national attitudes and preferences, it cannot be the logic of the ballot box alone that is to blame.

There is of course force in this point. It would be idle to deny that national experiences condition national attitudes differently and that these differences can affect the speed with which objective contradictions in politico-economic systems work themselves out.

Germany's experience of hyperinflation under the Weimar Republic and of the terrible political traumas that followed it certainly created a predisposition against inflation. Even as recently as 1967, this led the West German trade unions to reject as inflationary an all-'round wage increase that the then Minister of Economics, Karl Schiller, had proposed as a method of stimulating purchasing power in the depressed German economy.

But the interesting thing to note here is that it was not the political process that stood in the way of inflationary collective bargaining or that kept the natural rate of unemployment so low. It was a matter of attitudes expressed through industrial behavior. Moreover, these attitudes have not proved to be proof against the progression toward more rapid inflation, which in this essay is argued to be characteristic of democracies with free collective bargaining.

The case of the United States is more difficult. Although the same progression is visible, it has been argued above that American political institutions combined with American political priorities, as well as a lower degree of unionization, may mean that the United States will draw back from the final plunge into hyperinflation. This is indeed to concede that preferences expressed through the ballot box can, at least as a last resort, be brought to coincide with economic imperatives before disaster strikes.

Consistency must rest either on conceding that the United States is as doomed as the Western European industrialized democracies, or by allowing that the contradiction between political and economic imperatives is not necessarily an absolute, but merely an obtrusive and powerful tendency that predisposes all toward accelerating inflation and threatens all but the most robust with collapse. The latter certainly brings our thesis into better line with the nature of historical tendencies (which are seldom wholly mechanistically determined) and probably fits the facts of American and Western European experience better.

No mention has been made so far of the "socialist" alternative. This is much favored by those in Western Europe who would accept most of the foregoing analysis, but see it as fulfilling the collapse of capitalism rather than the more general collapse of any civilized attempt to combine a high degree of prosperity with a high degree of personal freedom. There is not space in this essay to investigate such an alternative.

But suffice it to say that any alternative must either seek

to work through the basic principles of liberal economics, acknowledging the role of prices in balancing supply and demand, or try to override them, presumably substituting either commands or spontaneous altruism by all economic units. The first approach must confront the same difficulties as we face now. The second leads in one form to totalitarianism—and great inefficiency—and in its other form to paradise. So far the only road to paradise that has not yet been proved to lead somewhere quite different lies through the grave.

Socialism: Obituary for an Idea

Irving Kristol

It used to be said that when ideas died in Europe, they came to the United States to be born again. There was much truth in this sardonic judgment of the United States as a second-rate intellectual power—and, alas, there is still much truth in it. As evidence, one can point to what has happened to American liberalism over these past twenty-five years. This liberalism has, with considerable effort, converted itself into a kind of neosocialism. We disguise this event from ourselves by our insistence on applying the term "liberal" to people who have long since abandoned most liberal beliefs in favor of the essential socialist principle—that is, the priority of equality over liberty. There is little doubt that our leading liberals, did they live in Western Europe, would be voting for the British Labour Party or the French Socialist Party or the German Social Democratic Party. Moreover, there can be little doubt that the kind of "restructuring" of American society envisioned by American liberals—the "reordering of our priorities," as they so gently put it—has the intention of remaking the United States in the image of European social democracy. And this at a time when that social democracy gives every sign of being intellectually and morally bankrupt, when it is retreating in disarray from its own principles, and when it has lost much of its credibility among those sections of the electorate that habitually supported it. Once again, our most "progressive" thinkers are constructing their platforms out of the debris of European history.

Though one wouldn't know it from the prevailing liberal rhetoric, the most important political event of the twentieth century is not the crisis of capitalist reality but the death of the socialist ideal. It is an event of immense significance, for with the passing of the socialist ideal there is removed from the political horizon the one alternative to capitalism that was rooted in the Judaeo-Christian tradition, and in the Western civilization that emerged from that tradition. Now, to ever greater degree, anticapitalism is becoming synonymous with one form or another of barbarism and tyranny. (Such, of course, is the case with the powerful Communist parties of Italy and France, which are certainly anticapitalist but which have long since ceased to have any serious intellectual or moral transactions with the socialist ideal.) And since capitalism, after two hundred or so years, is bound to endure crises and breed disaffection, it is nothing short of a tragedy that anticapitalist dissent should now be liberated from a socialist tradition which—one sees it clearly in perspective—had the function of civilizing dissent, a function it was able to perform because it implicitly shared so many crucial values with the liberal capitalism it opposed.

Today we live in a world with an ever-increasing number of people who call themselves socialists, an ever-increasing number of political regimes that call themselves socialist, but where the socialist ideal itself has been voided of all meaning and frequently of all humane substance as well. It must be emphasized that this is not a question of the institutional reality diverging markedly from the original inspiring ideal—as the Christian Church, let us say, diverged from the original vision of the Gospels. That kind of wayward development is natural and inevitable, if always dismaying—ideals pay a large price for their incarnation. In the case of contemporary socialism, however, the ideal itself has ceased to be of any interest to anyone—it has not been adapted to reality but contemptuously repudiated by it.

True, there is a dwindling band of socialist fideists who keep insisting that we must not judge socialism by any of its works. The Soviet Union, they tell us, is not "socialist" at all; nor is China, or Yugoslavia, or Cuba, or Hungary, or all those other "people's democracies." Neither, of course, are such regimes as exist in Peru or Syria or Zaïre, whose claims to socialist legitimacy are not to be taken seriously. As for Western countries with social-democratic governments, such as Britain or Sweden—well, they get a passing grade for "effort," but it seems that they are insufficiently resolute or intelligent to bring "true" socialism about.

This is all quite ridiculous, of course. Socialism is what socialism does. The plaintive lament of the purist that socialism (or capitalism, or Christianity) has "never really been tried" is simply the expression of petulance and obstinacy on the part of ideologues who, convinced that they have a more profound understanding than anyone else of the world and its history, now find that they have been living a huge self-deception. People who persist in calling themselves socialist, while decrying the three quarters of the world that has proclaimed itself socialist, and who can find a socialist country nowhere but in their imaginings—such people are anachronisms. As such they do serve a purpose: They help the historian and scholar understand what socialists used to think socialism was all about. One could discover that from reading books, to be sure, but it is sometimes enlightening to interview an actual survivor.

The absolute contradiction between the socialist reality today and the orginal socialist ideal is most perfectly revealed by the utter refusal of socialist collectivities even to think seriously about that ideal. Perhaps the most extraordinary fact of twentieth-century intellectual history is that all thinking about socialism takes place in nonsocialist countries. In this respect, one can once again see the fallacy in the analogy—so frequently and glibly made—between contemporary socialism and early Christianity. The Church certainly did deviate from the original teachings of Jesus and his apostles, and did transform these teachings into a theology suitable for an institutional religion. But these deviations and transformations, this development of Christian doctrine, were the work of the Church Fathers, whose powerful minds can fascinate us even today. In the case of contemporary socialism, there are no Church Fathers—only heretics, outside the reach of established orthodoxies, developing doctrines for which socialist authority has no use at all. Not a single interesting work on Marxism—not even an authoritative biography of Karl Marx!—has issued from the Soviet Union in its sixty years of existence. If you want to study Marxism, and meet Marxist intellectuals, you go to Paris, or Rome, or London, or some American university campus. There are no intellectual hegiras to Moscow, Peking, or Havana. Moreover, the works of these Western Marxist thinkers—and some of them are indeed impressive —are suppressed in socialist lands. Sartre's Marxist writings have never been published in the Soviet Union, just as Brecht's plays have never been produced there, and just as Picasso's paintings have never been exhibited there. Socialism, apparently, is one of those ideals which, when breathed upon by reality, suffers immediate petrifaction. Which is why all those who remain loyal to this ideal will always end up bewailing another "revolution betrayed."

The inevitable question is: What was the weakness at the heart of this ideal that has made it so vulnerable to reality? But in an obituary, it is indelicate to begin with the deceased's flaws of mind and character. It is more appropriate to take cognizance of, and pay one's respects to, his positive qualities. And the socialist ideal was, in many respects, an admirable one. More than that, it was a *necessary* ideal, offering elements that were wanting in capitalist society— elements indispensable for the preservation, not to say perfection, of our humanity.

The basic defects of a liberal-capitalist society have been obscured from us by the socialist critique itself—or, to be more precise, by the versions of this critique that ultimately became the intellectual orthodoxy of the socialist movements. The original sources of socialist dissent are best discovered by going back to the original socialists: the so-called "utopian" socialists, as distinguished from the later "scientific" socialists. Reading them, one finds that socialism derived its spiritual energy from a profound dissatisfaction, not with one or another aspect of liberal modernity, but with that modernity itself. Indeed, the original socialist criticism of the bourgeois world was, to a remarkable degree, a secular version of the indictment that the "reactionary" Catholic Church was then continually making, though to a world increasingly deaf to Christian tonalities.

The essential point of this indictment was that *liberty was not enough.* A society founded solely on "individual rights" was a society that ultimately deprived men of those virtues that could exist only in a *political community,* which is something other than a "society." Among these virtues are a sense of distributive justice, a fund of shared moral values, and a common vision of the good life sufficiently attractive and powerful to transcend the knowledge that each individual's life ends only in death. Capitalist society itself —as projected, say, in the writings of John Locke and Adam Smith—was negligent of such virtues. It did not reject them and in no way scorned them, but simply assumed that the individual would be able to cope with this matter as he did with his other "private" affairs. This assumption, in turn, was possible only because the founders of capitalism took it for granted that the moral and spiritual heritage of Judaism and Christianity was unassailable, and that the new individualism of bourgeois society would not "liberate" the individual from this tradition. It might free him from a particular theology, or a particular church; but he would "naturally" rediscover for himself, within himself, those values previously associated with that theology or church. This was very much a Protestant conception of the relation between men and the values by which they lived and died. It survived so long as traditional religious habits of mind survived in the individualist, secularized society of bourgeois capitalism. Which is to say, for many generations capitalism was able to live off the accumulated moral and spiritual capital of the past. But with each generation, that capital stock was noticeably depleted, had to be stretched ever thinner to meet the exigencies of life. Bankruptcy was inevitable, and we have seen it come in our own time, as a spirit of nihilism has dismissed not only the answers derived from tradition but also the very meaningfulness of the questions to which tradition provided the answers. A "good life" has thus come to signify a satisfactory "life style"—just another commodity that capitalism, in its affluence and generosity, makes available in a thousand assorted varieties, to suit a thousand tastes.

Socialism can be seen, in retrospect, to have been a kind of rebellion against the possibilities of nihilism inherent in the bourgeois Protestant principle—an effort, within the framework of modernity, to reconstruct a political community that would withstand the corruptions of modernity itself. To call it a "secular religion" is not far off the mark, and most of the original "utopian" socialists would have found nothing arguable in this ascription. The Saint-Simonians, as we know, very consciously set out to establish a post-Christian religion that preserved the best of

Christianity, as they understood it. All the utopian socialist communities had a religious core—at the very least, a "religion of humanity"—into whose values young people were indoctrinated. To challenge or criticize those values, and the way of life associated with them, was to risk immediate expulsion. In our own time, the Israeli kibbutz can remind us of what a socialist community, in the original sense, was supposed to be like.

This "utopian" socialism was not really "utopian" at all. Indeed, it is the only kind of socialism that has ever worked. The trouble is that it can only work under certain very restricted conditions: 1. The people who set out to create a socialist community must sincerely subscribe to socialist beliefs. 2. They must be satisfied with a *small* community; otherwise there will be division of labor, bureaucracy, social classes—in short, a "society" rather than a community. 3. They must be fairly indifferent to material goods, so that a *voluntary* equality will easily prevail. In circumstances such as these, socialist communities do "work," in the sense of continuing to exist and continuing to hold onto the loyalties of a new generation as well as those of the founding members. They work most effectively, as historians of socialism are fond of pointing out, when the religious core is strongest, because then the shared values are most successfully affirmed and reaffirmed. It is not an accident, after all, that the Greek *polis*—the model of political community—neither believed in nor practiced religious toleration, to say nothing of religious pluralism.

But this kind of socialism has always been marginal to socialist history, which had much larger ambitions. The "scientific socialism" of Marx and his followers—whether they defined themselves as "orthodox" Marxists, "neo"-Marxists, "revisionist" Marxists, or whatever—aimed to transform all of society, and quickly. It derided the idea of slowly converting people to a belief in socialism, until these people formed a majority. Similarly, it contemptuously rejected the notion of creating model socialist communities within the womb of capitalist society—as, say, the early Christians created their own exemplary communities throughout the Roman Empire. Though the moral and spiritual impetus toward socialism may have been derived —and is still largely derived—from a profound sense of the inadequacy of modernity to satisfy the yearnings for political community, postutopian socialism itself has become a modernist political doctrine. This is true of both the Communist and social-democratic versions of "scientific socialism," each of which, in its own way, takes a "managerial" and manipulative approach to politics and tries to create a new political community through the actions of government upon an unenlightened and recalcitrant populace.

The crucial difference between "scientific" socialism and "utopian" socialism lay in their attitudes toward economic growth and material prosperity. The "utopians" were not much interested in affluence, as we have come to understand that term—that is, an ever-increasing amount and variety of consumers' goods made available to an ever-increasing proportion of the population. They were by no means Spartan in their conception of a good community. They *did* expect to abolish poverty and to achieve a decent degree of material comfort, which would be equally shared. But their conception of a "decent" standard of living was, by twentieth-century standards, quite modest. This modesty was a matter of principle: Being community-oriented rather than individual-oriented, "utopian" socialism saw no merit in the constant excitation of individual appetites, which would inevitably place severe strains on the bonds of community. The main function of the socialist community, as they conceived it, was to produce a socialist type of individual—persons who had transcended the vulgar, materialistic, and divisive acquisitiveness that characterized the capitalist type of individual. Here again, the Israeli kibbutz gives us an insight into the "utopian" intention. The kibbutz aims to satisfy all the basic economic needs of the community, and even to achieve a pleasing level of comfort for its membership. But "affluence," in the sense of widespread individual possession of such "luxuries" as automobiles, television sets, hi-fi radios and record players, freezers and refrigerators, travel abroad, etc., is solemnly regarded as a political threat, to be coped with cautiously and prudently.

"Scientific socialism," in contrast, denounced capitalism for failing to produce the society of abundance made possible by modern technology, and mocked at "utopian" socialism for wishing to curb "needs" rather than satisfying them copiously. This approach made it possible for "scientific" socialism to become the basis of a mass movement, since it pandered so explicitly to the mass appetites excited—but also, to some degree, at any particular moment, frustrated —by capitalism. The political mass movements that had socialist goals then divided into two kinds: those that thought a liberal parliamentary democracy should be preserved within a socialist community, and those that thought this both unrealistic and undesirable. In the twentieth century, both these movements succeeded in establishing themselves as the governments of major nations. And in all such instances, the end result has been frustration and disillusionment.

In the case of totalitarian socialism—that current of socialist thought for which Lenin stands to Marx as St. Paul did to Jesus—the frustration has been absolute and definitive. Central economic planning of a rigorous kind has demonstrated a radical incapacity to cope with a complex industrialized economy and urbanized society. Obviously, the central planners can do certain things—that is, build steel mills or dams or armament factories. But the Pharaohs of ancient Egypt could boast of comparable achievements—there is nothing "socialist" about the ability of an all-powerful state to get certain things done. What the central planners of the Soviet Union clearly cannot do is to create an "affluent" society in which its citizens would have a standard of living on the level of that of Western Europe and the United States. The immense bureaucracy involved in such planning simply cannot compete with the free market as an efficient mechanism for allocating resources, nor is bureaucratic caution able to substitute for entre-preneurial risk-taking as a mechanism of innovation and economic growth.

Yet a Western standard of "affluence" is precisely what the Soviet citizens want. These citizens never were "so-cialists" in any meaningful sense of that term, nor have sixty years of Communist rule succeeded in making them such. In the earlier decades of the Soviet regime there was a lot of windy talk about "the new Soviet Man" who would emerge from "the Soviet experiment." One hears little such prattle today, even from official Soviet sources. Soviet com-munism is a pseudoreligion, and the Soviet Government is a pseudotheocracy which, even after decades of coercion and terror, has been pitifully unable to effect any kind of mass conversion to socialist beliefs. As has been noted, there are no socialist intellectuals in the Soviet Union—only an in-creasing number of antisocialist intellectuals. The effort to create a socialist society that would be more prosperous, more "affluent," than a capitalist one, while creating a socialist citizenry through unremitting *force majeure,* has been a disastrous failure. "Managerial" socialism has turned out to be far more utopian than "utopian" socialism.

The same destiny has awaited the non-Leninist, social-democratic version of "managerial" socialism. Where one can claim success for it, it is a success that is a kind of failure in socialist terms. Such is the case of Sweden, after decades of social-democratic government. It has been a prosperous country, with a healthy economy and a stable society—but its economy and society can be fairly described as "mixed," that is, half private capitalism, half state capitalism. Those Swedes who still think of themselves as socialists are intensely dissatisfied with this state of affairs, and are constantly urging the government toward greater state control and a more egalitarian distribution of income. Since the Swedish Social Democrats are still officially committed to the socialist ideal, they find it impossible to resist this ideological pressure. The drift is unremittingly toward the "left," and would have remained so, had not the Social Democrats been voted out of office. The consequences of any such socialist drift would have been entirely predictable: slower economic growth, higher inflation, and lower productivity—all amid increasing popular discontent that could not be calmed by a more punitive and egalitarian tax system. Egalitarianism, in Sweden, does not reflect any sincere, personal commitment on the part of the Swedish people to the ideal of equality. It is, rather, a strategy whereby organized labor on the one hand, and the state bureaucracy on the other, receive an ever-increasing share of the national income and of political power. This appetite will not be appeased by a more equal distribution of income or wealth. The demand for "more"—not for "more equal," but for "more"—will feed upon itself, until an economic, and eventually political, crisis either creates an authoritarian regime that copes with discontent by repressing it or provokes a reversion to a more liberal-capitalist economic order.

In a sense, Great Britain represents Sweden's "socialist" future. Though Britain's movement toward "socialism" came much later than Sweden's, and though some of the more conservative British socialists still talk as if a Swedish condition were the ultimate ideal they were striving for, the British impulse has been more powerful, less controllable, less deferential toward economic realities. There has been more nationalization of industry in Britain, the trade unions are far more belligerent, and the "left" socialists—the ideological fanatics who redouble their socialist efforts as the socialist ends fade into unreality—are more influential. The consequences for the British economy have been disastrous—Britain now vies with Italy for the title "the sick man of Europe"—and there have been no discernible compensating improvements in the British social and political order. No one even seriously claims that the British people are in any sense "happier" as a result of their socialist experiences. Indeed, all the objective indices of social pathology —crime, juvenile delinquency, corruption, ethnic dissent, emigration, etc.—show steady increases.

It is hard to believe that Britain will simply continue on this downward course. The British love of liberty is still strong, the British liberal political tradition still possesses a large degree of popular acceptance, the British people as a whole are still more reliant on common sense than they are enamored of political fantasies. It is reasonable to expect that the Labour government will be succeeded by a Conservative government, and that the British experience with socialism will be followed by a "reactionary" affirmation of the principles of liberal capitalism. But then the issue will be posed anew: What can a liberal capitalist society do to inoculate itself against a resurgence of anticapitalist dissent?

We now know a part of that answer. One of the things that can be done is to design all measures of "social welfare" so as to maintain the largest degree of individual choice. The demand for a "welfare state" is, on the part of the majority of the people, a demand for a greater minimum of political community, for more "social justice" (that is, distributive justice) than capitalism, in its pristine,

individualistic form, can provide. It is not at all a demand
for "socialism," or anything like it. Nor is it really a
demand for intrusive government by a powerful and ubiq-
uitous bureaucracy—though that is how socialists and neo-
socialists prefer to interpret it. Practically all of the really
popular demands and truly widespread support for a "welfare state" would be satisfied by a mixture of voluntary and
compulsory insurance schemes—old-age insurance, disability insurance, unemployment insurance, medical insurance
—that are reasonably (if not perfectly) compatible with a
liberal capitalist society. Over the past quarter century, a
host of "conservative" and "neoconservative" economists
and social critics have showed us how such mechanisms
could and would work, and their intellectual victory over
earlier "Fabian" conceptions of social reform has been decisive. The problem, at the moment, is to persuade the
business community and the "conservative" (that is, antisocialist) political parties of their practicality. Not an
easy mission, but not in principle an intractable one.

Other problems indigenous to a liberal capitalist society
are still virgin territory so far as constructive theory is concerned. What, for instance, shall we do about the government of those most peculiar capitalist institutions, the large
corporations—bureaucratic (and, in a sense, "collectivist") versions of capitalist enterprise that Adam Smith
would surely have detested? And, even more important,
what can a liberal capitalist society do about the decline of
religious beliefs and traditional values—a decline or-
ganically rooted in liberal capitalism's conception of this
realm as an essentially "private affair," neither needing nor
meriting public sanction? These and other questions will
continue to make any "counterreformation" on the part of
liberal capitalism an exceedingly fragile enterprise. But
they will have to be answered if the death of socialism is
not simply to mean a general disintegration into pseudoso-

cialist political forms whose only common element is a repudiation in the name of "equality," of individual liberty as a prime political value.

As Cardinal Newman once observed, it is not too hard to show the flaws in any system of thought, religious or political, but an erroneous idea can be expelled from the mind only by the active presence of another idea. The dead idea of socialism is now putrefying both the world's mind and the world's body. It has to be removed and buried—with appropriate honors, if that will help. Ironically, only liberal capitalism can perform that funereal task.

Notes

THE INFIRMITY OF BRITISH MEDICINE

Harry Schwartz

1. *Sunday Times* (London) (Oct. 12, 1975), p. 6.
2. *New Scientist* (Aug. 21, 1975), pp. 410–11.
3. *British Medical Journal* (Dec. 12, 1942), p. 700.
4. Quoted in Paul F. Gemmill, *Britain's Search for Health* (Philadelphia: University of Pennsylvania Press, 1960), p. 20.
5. Quoted in Michael Foot, *Aneurin Bevan: A Biography* (New York: Atheneum, 1974), Vol. 2, p. 191.
6. Ibid., p. 138.
7. Ibid., p. 213.
8. Aneurin Bevan, *In Place of Fear* (New York: Monthly Review Press, 1964) p. 107.
9. Foot, op. cit., pp. 252–53.
10. John and Sylvia Jewkes, *Value for Money in Medicine* (Oxford: Basil Blackwell, 1963), pp. 59–60.
11. Rosemary Stevens, *Medical Practice in Modern England.* (New Haven and London: Yale University Press, 1966), p. 208. *British Medical Journal* (Dec. 13, 1975), p. 656.
12. Jewkes and Jewkes, op. cit., p. 55.
13. Information gathered in London in September 1976.
14. *Times* (London) (June 19, 1975), p. 4.
15. *British Medical Journal* (Mar. 22, 1975), p. 678.
16. Ibid.
17. *New England Journal of Medicine* (May 8, 1975), p. 1036.
18. *British Medical Journal* (June 7, 1975), pp. 571–72.
19. Rudolf Klein, "Private Practice," *New Society* (Oct. 23, 1975), p. 215.
20. *British Medical Journal* (Dec. 6, 1975), p. 542.

CRIME AND PUNISHMENT IN ENGLAND

James Q. Wilson

1. American data on crime, here and elsewhere in text, from Federal Bureau of Investigation, *Uniform Crime Reports,* 1973 (Washington,

D.C.: U. S. Government Printing Office); British data from Government Statistical Service, *Social Trends*, No. 5 (1974) (London: Her Majesty's Stationery Office).

2. F. H. McClintock and N. Howard Avison, *Crime in England and Wales* (London: Heinemann, 1968), p. 55.

3. Colin Greenwood, *Firearms Control* (London: Routledge & Kegan Paul, 1972), p. 165. See also Greenwood, "Controlling Violent Crime," *New Society* (May 31, 1973), pp. 491ff.

4. Greenwood, Chap. 11.

5. M. J. Pratt, "Robbery and Kindred Offenses in the Metropolitan Police District, 1968–1972," mimeo by London Metropolitan Police Statistical Unit C11 (Jan. 1973).

6. McClintock and Avison, pp. 23–24.

7. *Social Trends*, pp. 83–84.

8. *Social Trends*, p. 84.

9. McClintock and Avison, p. 245.

10. U.S. data from *Statistical Abstract*, 1972, p. 30; British data from *Social Trends*, p. 75.

11. *Social Trends*, p. 189.

12. *Social Trends*, p. 100.

13. *Social Trends*, p. 114.

14. See the summary of this literature in John B. Mays, *Crime and Its Treatment*, 2nd ed. (London: Longman, 1975). pp. 62–69.

15. Mays, pp. 70–74.

16. *Social Trends*, p. 81.

17. Leslie Wilkins, "What is Crime?" *New Society* (July 18, 1963), quoted in Mays, p. 20.

18. McClintock and Avison, Chap. 4.

19. *Report of the Commissioner of Police of the Metropolis for the Year 1974*, Cmnd. 6068 (London: HMSO, 1975), p. 19.

20. Home Office, *Judges' Rules and Administrative Directions to the Police* (London: HMSO, 1964), Appendix B, Sec. 7 (a).

21. R. M. Jackson, *Enforcing the Law*, rev. ed. (London: Penguin Books, 1972), p. 121.

22. *Report of the Commissioner*, p. 38.

23. *Report of the Commissioner*, p. 111.

24. *Report of the Commissioner*, pp. 112–13.

25. Speech given by the Commissioner of Police of the Metropolis at Bramshill College (Aug. 14, 1975) (mimeo), p. 3.

26. Ibid., p. 4.

27. Quoted in Michael Cockerell, "How Good Is Scotland Yard Now?" *The Listener* (Feb. 6, 1975).

28. Ibid.

29. Robert Mark, "Minority Verdict," the 1973 Dimbleby Lecture on the British Broadcasting Corporation (Nov. 6, 1973), and interview with Kenneth Harris in *The Observer* (Mar. 23, 1975).

30. *Statistical Abstract, 1972,* p. 160. Excludes those held in jails and juvenile facilities.
31. *Social Trends,* p. 195. Excludes those held in Borstals and detention centers and those awaiting trial.
32. There were 7,465 reported robberies and 1,915 persons confined in 1971. *Criminal Statistics in England and Wales,* Cmnd. 5020 (London: HMSO, 1972), calculated from Tables I (a) and II (a).
33. There were 41,397 reported robberies and 1,653 persons confined on conviction of that charge. Bureau of Criminal Statistics, Department of Justice, *Crime and Delinquency in California, 1970* (Sacramento, Calif.). Calculated from Tables I-11 and III-18.
34. Roger Hood and Richard Sparks, *Key Issues in Criminology* (London: Weidenfeld and Nicolson, 1972), p. 142.
35. Hood and Sparks, pp. 147–51.
36. Richard F. Sparks, *Local Prisons: The Crisis in the English Penal System* (London: Heinemann, 1971), p. 89.
37. Quoted in *New Society* (Dec. 13, 1973), p. 662.
38. Quoted in *Daily Telegraph* (Mar. 26, 1970).
39. Sparks, p. 91.
40. Sparks, p. 89.
41. Sparks, p. 105.
42. The studies are summarized in James Q. Wilson, *Thinking About Crime* (New York: Basic Books, 1975), pp. 169–70.
43. See the review of the Younger Committee Report by Roger Hood, *British Journal of Criminology* (Oct. 1974), pp. 388–95.
44. Quoted in *LEAA Newsletter,* Vol. 5, No. 3 (Sept.–Oct. 1975) (publication of the Law Enforcement Assistance Administration of the U. S. Department of Justice), p. 3.
45. Roger Hood, "Tolerance and the Tariff," address to the National Association for the Care and Resettlement of Offenders (London, July 1974).
46. *Social Trends,* p. 186.

THE FAILURE OF THE CONSERVATIVE PARTY, 1945–75

Patrick Cosgrave

1. Robert Blake, *The Conservative Party from Peel to Churchill,* based on the Ford Lectures delivered before the University of Oxford in the Hilary Term of 1968 (London, 1970).
2. T. F. Lindsay and Michael Harrington, *The Conservative Party 1918–70* (London, 1974). There is nothing really comprehensive on the recent history of the Conservative Party, but this book contains the

truest generalizations and is worth the attention of every student of the subject.

3. At the outset of the Suez operation Mr. Macmillan was enthusiastic for its prosecution, and this earned him a right-wing reputation. Subsequently he was most anxious for its abandonment.

4. London, 1971.

WELFARE IN THE WELFARE STATE

Leslie Lenkowsky

1. Andrew Shonfield, *British Economic Policy Since the War* (London: Penguin Books, 1958), p. 58.
2. Beatrice Webb, *Our Partnership* (London: Longmans, Green and Co., 1948), p. 479.
3. "They Don't Work Hard Enough," *The Economist* (Dec. 20, 1975), p. 78.
4. Sir William Beveridge, *Social Insurance and Allied Services* (Cmnd. 6404) (London, 1942), p. 6.
5. Roger Lawson and Bruce Reed, *Social Security in the European Community*, PEP (London, 1975), p. 32.
6. "Welfare in a Cold Climate," *The Economist* (Sept. 20, 1975), p. 46.
7. Edgar K. Browning, *Redistribution and the Welfare System*, (Washington, D.C.: American Enterprise Institute, 1975), p. 16.
8. Lawson and Reed, p. 21.
9. "Life on the Dole," *The Economist* (Mar. 1, 1975), p. 34.
10. Odin W. Anderson, *Health Care: Can There Be Equity?* (New York: John Wiley & Sons), p. 225.
11. Roger Lawson, "EEC Benefits," *New Society* (Mar. 29, 1973), p. 701.
12. "Report," *New Society* (Jan. 8, 1976), p. 57.
13. Bernard Weinraub, "Swedes Discuss the Impact of Welfare System on Freedom," the New York *Times* (Nov. 12, 1972), p. 28. In 1976 the Swedish Social Democratic Party, which developed the welfare state, lost its majority in the Riksdag after four decades of continuous rule.
14. Rudolf Klein, ed., *Inflation and Priorities* (London: Centre for Studies in Social Policy, 1975), p. 14.
15. Ibid., Chap. 1.
16. Government Statistical Service, *Social Trends*, No. 4 (London: HMSO, 1973), p. 203.
17. Klein, p. 16.
18. *Social Trends*, p. 203.
19. Frank Blackaby, "The Living Standard," *New Society* (Oct. 17, 1974), p. 150.

20. H. A. Turner and Frank Wilkinson, "The Seventh Pay Policy," *New Society* (July 17, 1975), p. 136.
21. "The Days of Creeping Socialism," *The Economist* (July 6, 1974), p. 70.
22. "Report," *New Society* (Dec. 12, 1974), p. 688.
23. Rudolf Klein, "Private Practice," *New Society* (Oct. 23, 1975), p. 215.
24. *Social Trends,* p. 110.
25. Thomas Acton, "Charities and the Iron Law of Chaos," *New Society* (Nov. 21, 1974), p. 477.
26. "The Days of Creeping Socialism," p. 71.
27. John Coyne, "Social Wage," *New Society* (May 8, 1975), p. 340.
28. Rudolf Klein, "Expenditure," *New Society* (Feb. 6, 1975), p. 323.
29. Royal Commission on the Distribution of Income and Wealth (Diamond Commission), *Initial Report on the Standing Reference,* Report No. 1 (Cmnd. 6171) (London, 1975), Table 15, p. 45.
30. Op. cit.
31. Op. cit.
32. Op. cit. "Middle" and "upper-middle" classes refer to households in the eleventh through fiftieth percentiles.
33. Ibid., Table 24, p. 62.
34. George Polanyi and John B. Wood, *How Much Inequality?* (London: Institute of Economic Affairs, 1974), Table 13, p. 48.
35. A. B. Atkinson, *The Economics of Inequality* (Oxford: Clarendon Press, 1975), Table 4.4, p. 68.
36. Diamond Commission, Table 15, p. 45.
37. Ibid., Table 25, p. 64.
38. Ibid., Table 41, p. 97.
39. Ibid., Table 45, p. 102. These estimates are derived from slightly different assessments. Using the same technique as in 1973, the share of the top 1 per cent in 1960 was 38.2 per cent.
40. Op. cit.
41. Ibid., Table 48, p. 107.
42. Ibid., Table 39, p. 92.
43. "Europe Report," *New Society* (May 8, 1975), pp. 346–47.
44. "Report," *New Society* (Nov. 6, 1975), pp. 319–20.
45. Ibid., p. 320.
46. Alan Maynard and Arthur Walker, "Cutting Public Spending," *New Society* (Dec. 4, 1975), p. 529.
47. "Report," *New Society* (Nov. 6, 1975), p. 320.
48. "Europe Report," p. 347. See also Robert Bacon and Walter Eltis, *Britain's Economic Problem: Too Few Producers* (London: Macmillan, 1976).
49. See Rudolf Klein, Martin Buxton, and Quentin Outram, *Constraints and Choices* (London: Centre for Studies in Social Policy, 1976).
50. "Report," *New Society* (Nov. 6, 1975), p. 319.

51. See Adam Ridley, "The Problem of Public Expenditure," Conservative Research Department (London, Feb. 1976). Mr. Ridley is an adviser to Margaret Thatcher.
52. See Edmund Dell, *Political Responsibility and Industry* (London: George Allen and Unwin, 1974).
53. Ralph Harris and Arthur Seldon, *Choice in Welfare 1970* (London: Institute of Economic Affairs, 1971), Table 1, p. 19.
54. Quoted in "Some Carve-up, Some Cake," *The Economist* (Feb. 21, 1976), p. 73.

About the Contributors

THE UNITED STATES

Irving Kristol is Henry R. Luce Professor of Urban Values at New York University and co-editor of *The Public Interest*. He contributes a regular column to the *Wall Street Journal* and is the author of *On the Democratic Idea in America* (1972).

Leslie Lenkowsky is Director of Research for the Smith Richardson Foundation. He is writing his Harvard doctoral dissertation of "The Politics of Welfare in the United States and Britain" and has been a research assistant with Daniel Patrick Moynihan and assistant to the Secretary of Public Welfare for the state of Pennsylvania. His articles have appeared in *Commentary, The New Leader,* and *The Alternative.*

Harry Schwartz, Distinguished Professor at the State University College, New Paltz, N.Y., is also on the editorial board of the New York *Times.* His books include *Tsars, Mandarins and Commissars* (1973), *The Case for American Medicine* (1972), *Prague's 200 Days* (1969), and *An Introduction to the Soviet Economy* (1968).

R. Emmett Tyrrell, Jr., is editor-in-chief of *The Alternative: An American Spectator,* a journal of opinion published in Bloomington, Indiana. He has also written for *Harper's, Commentary, National Review,* the New York *Times,* and the *Wall Street Journal.*

James Q. Wilson is the Henry Lee Shattuck Professor of Government at Harvard. His books include *Thinking About Crime* (1975), *Political Organization* (1974), and, with Edward Banfield, *City Politics* (1963); his essays have appeared in many magazines and newspapers.

BRITAIN

Samuel Brittan is economic commentator of *The Financial Times* and a Visiting Fellow of Nuffield College, Oxford. He has previously worked on *The Observer* and was an adviser at the Department of Economic

Affairs. His books include *Capitalism and the Permissive Society* (1973) and (with Peter Lilley) *The Delusion of Incomes Policy* (1977).

Patrick Cosgrave writes for *The Spectator* and the London *Daily Telegraph*. He is the author of *Churchill at War* (Vol. 1, 1974) and *The Public Poetry of Robert Lowell* (1970).

Peter Jay is economics editor of *The Times* of London and has served in various government positions. In 1972 he wrote *The Budget*.

Colin Welch is deputy editor of the London *Daily Telegraph* and has contributed to the *New Statesman, Encounter,* and *The Spectator,* among other publications.

Peregrine Worsthorne is associate editor of the London *Sunday Telegraph* and has contributed to the *New Statesman, Encounter,* and *Foreign Affairs*. He is the author of *The Socialist Myth* (1971).

DATE DUE

HIGHSMITH 45-220